NE LYNCH · MICHAEL PETERSON · SI
ARROLL · MICK FANNIN
LER WRIGHT · MIDGE
SIMON ANDERSON · MARK RICHAR
DGE · LAYNE BEACHLEY · STEPH GIL
NAT YOUNG · WAYNE LYNCH · MICH
RICHARDS · TOM CARROLL · MICK F
EPH GILMORE · TYLER WRIGHT · M
MICHAEL PETERSON · SIMON AND
CK FANNING · PAM BURRIDGE · LAY
RIGHT · MIDGET FARRELLY · NAT YO
IMON ANDERSON · MARK RICHARD
DGE · LAYNE BEACHLEY · STEPH GIL
NAT YOUNG · WAYNE LYNCH · MICH
RICHARDS · TOM CARROLL · MICK F
EPH GILMORE · TYLER WRIGHT · M
MICHAEL PETERSON · SIMON AND
CK FANNING · PAM BURRIDGE · LAY
RIGHT · MIDGET FARRELLY · NAT YO
IMON ANDERSON · MARK RICHARD
DGE · LAYNE BEACHLEY · STEPH GIL
NAT YOUNG · WAYNE LYNCH · MICH

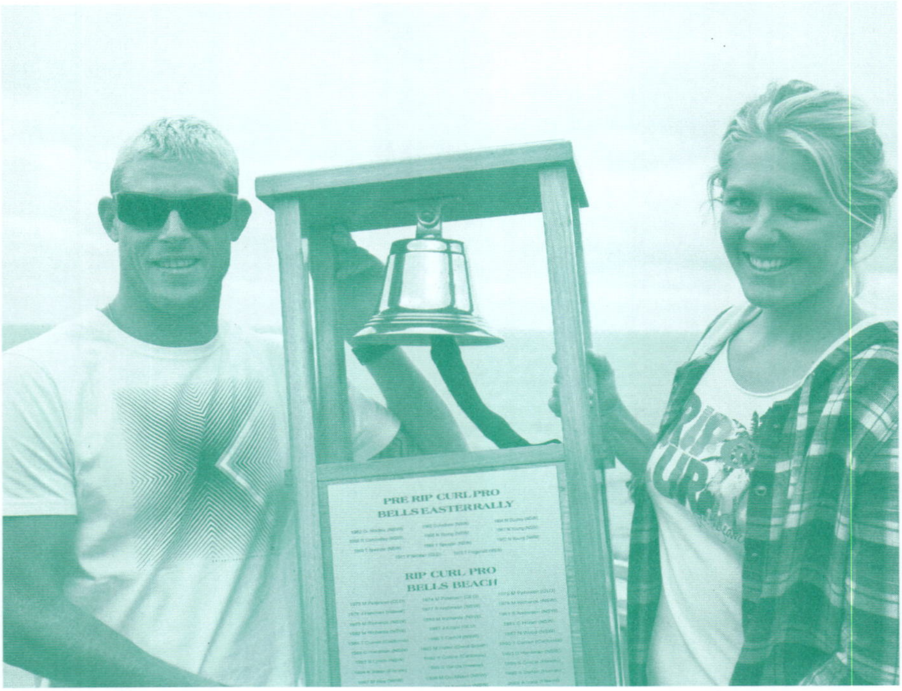
PRE RIP CURL PRO
BELLS EASTERRALLY
RIP CURL PRO
BELLS BEACH

The IMMORTALS
of Australian Surfing

Michael Peterson at the height of his mastery: the inaugural Stubbies Pro, Burleigh Heads, 1977. Photo dickhoole.com.au.

The
IMMORTALS
of Australian Surfing

Phil Jarratt

GELDING STREET PRESS

A Gelding Street Press book
An imprint of Rockpool Publishing

PO Box 252
Summer Hill
NSW 2130 Australia

www.geldingstreetpress.com

ISBN: 9780645207095

Published in Australia in 2023 by Rockpool Publishing

Copyright text © Phil Jarratt 2023
Copyright design © Rockpool Publishing 2023

Copyright all images © photographers as stated in each photo caption.
Major photographic supplier: Peter 'Joli' Wilson/Joli Productions.

Design and typesetting by Daniel Poole, Rockpool Publishing
Acquisition editor: Luke West, Rockpool Publishing
Edited by Lisa Macken

All rights reserved. No part of this publication may be reproduced, stored in a retrieval system or transmitted in any form or by any means, electronic, mechanical, photocopying, recording or otherwise, without the prior written permission of the publisher.

A catalogue record for this book is available from the National Library of Australia

Printed and bound in China

10 9 8 7 6 5 4 3 2 1

DEDICATION

In memory of the late, great Bobby Brown, who didn't live long enough to make the cut – which doesn't quite make sense, but if you knew him and surfed with him you'll know what I mean. And to Jackie, who just keeps putting up with my strange and disruptive obsession with surf. And to the gorgeous grandies, who need to read when they're not surfing and hopefully will.

Mick Fanning was crowned the 2009 ASP World Champion following a stunning performance at the Billabong Pipeline Masters at the Banzai Pipeline. Photo Joli.

CONTENTS

Introduction 1

THE IMMORTALS

    1.   Midget Farrelly 7

    2.   Nat Young 21

    3.   Wayne Lynch 35

    4.   Michael Peterson 49

    5.   Simon Anderson 63

    6.   Mark Richards 77

    7.   Tom Carroll 91

    8.   Mick Fanning 105

    9.   Pam Burridge 119

   10.   Layne Beachley 133

   11.   Steph Gilmore 147

   12.   Tyler Wright 161

Honourable mentions 174

Bibliography 194

Acknowledgements 197

About the author 199

Nat Young looking truly immortal, 1974. Photo Albe Falzon.

INTRODUCTION

I hope you, dear reader, will find this highly subjective selection of 12 of Australian surfing's Immortals entertaining because for me, as well as a modest fee, there's likely to be a punch in the face or three.

I have some experience of that which I speak. In a previous century my book-packaging consultancy in Sydney was selected to produce a huge book called *Australian Sporting Hall of Fame* for the Nine Network's *Wide World of Sports*. The selection of 50 titans of Australian sport was not done by any kind of viewer poll or democratic vote. No: it was decided that the two presenters of *Wide World of Sports*, Ian Chappell and Mike Gibson, plus my business partner and I would meet once a week until it was sorted.

Because there was likely to be some shouting and bad language involved Gibbo thought it would be best if we held our meetings on a boat, so it was agreed that once a week we would convene at the Mosman Rowing Club for a couple of mood enhancers then board a boat laden with cold beer and fresh oysters, drop anchor in a quiet cove and draw up our lists. It actually worked quite well: no one was thrown overboard, and even when we argued heatedly we'd kiss and make up over a nightcap at the Rowers.

Except this once. We had two allocations for men's tennis and 'Rocket' Rod Laver had a mortgage on one of them. Chappelli and I favoured John Newcombe for the other, and my partner Jamo was wavering. But Gibbo was adamant that Newk was just a show pony with a fancy moustache and that the spot must go to Ken 'Muscles' Rosewall. That was it: game, set and match. Thank you, linesmen, thank you, ball boys.

But it wasn't. Newk got the nod and Gibbo yelled at us all the way to the dock, then in the club he yelled and fumed some more. In his introduction to the book he wrote: 'I still can't understand how we left you out, Muscles. I was outvoted.' Okay, he never threw a punch, but until he died every time I encountered the great radio and TV man he'd say: 'You, ya bastard! You were the ringleader. I can't believe you left Muscles out.'

Wayne Lynch gliding at Mundaka, Spain in 1989. Photo Joli.

The odd thing is that over time I came to the conclusion that he was right, and as I put the finishing touches on this selection of surfing's Immortals I wonder how many people will rail at me for a tragic omission (or more) that will also turn out to be wrong.

The Immortals of Australian Surfing is the eighth book in Gelding Street Press's Immortals of Australian Sport series. Previous instalments focused on the greats of such sports as cricket, rugby league, motor racing, horse racing and soccer, each nominating a small group of individuals whose fame and feats are expected to endure forever.

It was the rough and tumble sport of rugby league that gave birth to the whole Immortals phenomenon, and the jacket blurb for *The Immortals of Australian Rugby League* briefly backgrounded that rare acknowledgement: 'The Immortals concept has become an established part of the Australian rugby league scene. It honours a very select group of former players regarded as the game's elite. These players weren't just high achievers and standout performers, but also influential identities who set a new benchmark and changed the way rugby league is played.'

To a large extent, the Australian Rugby League Commission's framework for bestowing Immortal status provides guiding principles for these books, but what exactly makes an Immortal? It varies from sport to sport, of course, and is an imprecise mix of fame, prodigious talent, competitive success, remarkable achievement and magnetism.

A sportsperson doesn't need to tick all of these boxes to be considered an Immortal, but being a household name is a very good start. However, it's not the be all and end all of immortality, as there are legendary figures who caused a significant shift in the way their chosen sport was played or approached who never reached the dizzying heights of others in competition.

Choosing a subjective list of the best in any sport is fraught with difficulty but it's particularly so in

Layne Beachley at Teahupo'o, Tahiti circa 2000. Photo Joli.

surfing, because even though we now have almost half a century of improving statistical information on the professional sport, competitive performance is only one part of the criteria by which surfers can be judged as being immortal. To use it as the sole criterion would be to ignore the opinions of a vast majority of lifelong, highly competent recreational or lifestyle surfers who choose not to compete and pay scant attention to the World Surf League, even when you can watch every heat on Fox Sports. To them, a brilliant surfer such as Wayne Lynch, who could beat the world's best in competition because he was one of them but who preferred the solitude of little-known, mid-ocean breaks that felt the full power of the Southern Ocean, easily trumps a surfer such as Michael Peterson, who lived and breathed to win contests. Both are in this book.

Likewise, it would be unwise to dismiss the excellent surfers who have taken a holistic approach to their sport and passion by designing the equipment they ride – which paradoxically was the reason Mark Richards won four world titles and Simon Anderson didn't win any – but they are both immortalised in these pages. In fact, I'm acutely aware that the holistic approach, when combined with the ability to win, is what drives surfing forward, sharing with the masses the drive power of the elite, so where tough choices needed to be made I have favoured it. Starting with our first world champion, the late Bernard 'Midget' Farrelly, at least half my Immortals are holistic surfers.

I wasn't given strict rules by the publisher so I didn't create any. I did, however, take the view (arguable, but only just) that the great advancement of modern Australian surfboard riding began after 1956, when a visiting Californian and Hawaiian lifeguard team introduced the finned Malibu Chip balsawood board. Pedants will argue that the Malibu Chip had actually been introduced to Australia six years earlier, when the Hollywood actor Peter Lawford rode his at Bondi before locking it in the surf club storage shed while he made the film *Kangaroo* in South Australia. Yes, but one person rode it once, and this does not a revolution make.

Likewise, there is a considerable history of surfboard riding in Australia over the first half of the 20th century, beginning a decade before Duke Kahanamoku's Sydney

Steph Gilmore heads out for her next encounter at Snapper Rocks, Queensland in 2011. Photo Joli.

exhibitions and continuing until barbed-wire barricades blocked our beaches for the duration of the Second World War. Interrupted by two great wars, advancement of the sport over this period never reached more than snail's pace.

There are more men than women in this collection because it's historic. Gender equality has come to our sport late but, boy, have we seen some warrior women emerge in recent years! I make no apologies for the sins of inequality of various governing bodies over many decades, other than to say I wish I'd been more inclusive back when we knew no better.

Finally, to the dear reader who might ask how does *he* get to choose? Luck of the draw, old sport, but as a lifelong surfer and archivist, historian and documentarian of it for more than 50 years, hopefully I bring some degree of perspective to the job at hand.

Phil Jarratt

Introduction · 5

Midget Farrelly at Whale Beach, Sydney, 1972. Photo Albe Falzon.

1

MIDGET FARRELLY

Full name	Bernard Farrelly
Nickname	Midget
Birthdate	13 September 1944; died 7 August 2016
Place of birth	Paddington, New South Wales

In becoming a champion he created a culture that has flourished over the decades and now outlives him.

Almost 60 years since he won surfing's first world title and a handful of years since his untimely death, the enigmatic 'Midget' Farrelly remains the best known of Australia's many surfing champions – not just because of his undoubted prowess on a surfboard, but also for the radical shift he represented in Australia's leisure culture.

For many baby boomers Midget was the surf craze, the icon of the new breed of youth who had turned their backs on a conventional working life to chase waves up and down the coast. In fact, throughout his life Farrelly took his job as a surfer and a surfboard designer more seriously than most nine to fivers did.

Bernard Farrelly was born in Paddington, a then working-class inner suburb of Sydney, on 13 September 1944, the first child of Irish and English immigrants. Farrelly Senior was by all accounts (and there aren't many) a somewhat sombre character who forever looked for the greener grass and became disillusioned when he didn't find it. He stayed in Sydney's Eastern Suburbs, however, and worked as a taxi driver while Bernard and second child Jane were tiny, somehow managing to save some money in those frugal, post-war years.

When Bernard was eight or nine the family lived by the beach at North Bondi and the young boy fell under the spell of an uncle,

Ray Hookham, who was a member of the surf club and an accomplished rider of the long toothpick boards. Farrelly recalled in 2012: 'Ever since I caught my first wave on the front of my uncle Ray's fourteen-foot hollow board at North Bondi at age six, I knew something special was in my future.'

Bernard had to put his new love on hold when his father announced that the family was going on an extended vacation abroad. En route to Canada, where they stayed for more than a year, the Farrellys spent some time in Waikiki. Bernard marvelled at the local beach boys riding their hot curl boards but didn't pluck up the courage to rent one and try it.

When the Farrellys finally returned to Sydney they set up home at Manly, where as Midget recalled in his 1965 book *This Surfing Life*: 'One day when I was down on the beach I came across a really huge, beat-up paddle board sitting on the sand just a few feet from the water. It was a monster – about seventeen feet long . . . there was no one around so I took this thing and pushed it out into the surf and tried to catch a wave . . . I didn't do very well at first but then I managed to catch a wave standing up. I guess I must have been pretty stoked.'

> 'Ever since I caught my first wave on the front of my uncle Ray's fourteen-foot hollow board . . . I knew something special was in my future.'

During the following year of 1956 Californian and Hawaiian lifeguards here for the Melbourne Olympics introduced the Malibu Chip surfboard to Australia, and everything changed. Farrelly saw the Americans on their balsa hotdoggers at Manly, but another summer passed before the spindly kid – who had been nicknamed 'Midget' because that's what he looked like on the toothpicks – swapped boards with another surfer. He recalled: 'I took off kneeling on this little thing, wondering what was going to happen. Suddenly the board turned sideways on me and I was travelling so fast across the wave that I was really startled.'

Midget scrimped and saved and bought himself one of the local variants on the Malibu Chip, a 10-feet plywood board that was hollow in the middle and had solid sides. Farrelly's teenage contemporaries remember him as being wry, witty and extremely resourceful, and he proved it by

The first Australian surf hero at Makaha, 1962. Photo Ron Church.

buying one of the first balsa blanks available in Sydney and teaching himself to shape and glass it in his Manly backyard. Proud of his work and his new nickname, Midget drew an oval decal with an 'M' at its centre and glassed it onto the deck.

In 1958 the Farrelly family moved inland to the suburb of Forestville, but Midget didn't spend a lot of time there. He had become a junior member of the Dee Why boys, a group of pioneer surfers who travelled as a pack along the length of the Northern Beaches peninsula. The surfers who mentored Midget during this period and got him odd jobs in the surfboard industry extended beyond the Dee Why boys and included Manly's Bob Pike, Dave Jackman (later famous for conquering the Queenscliff bombora), Mick Dooley, Joe Larkin, Bob Evans and the southside's Jack 'Bluey' Mayes.

It was home-movie buff Larkin who took Farrelly on his first real surf trip, to faraway Queensland, an experience Farrelly later claimed opened his eyes to a whole world of surf beyond Sydney. In 1958 Midget also entered his first surf contest, or 'rally' as these early meets were called. Held in chunky right-handers off the Avalon rock pool, the contest featured just about every serious surfer in Sydney. Midget made the final and finished fourth, but according to those who were there to witness it the smooth, flowing Farrelly style had yet to emerge.

By 1961, northside surfer Bob Evans had grown tired of distributing early surf movies from the US and decided to make his own. The entrepreneurial Evans, whose day job was selling women's lingerie, organised a cheap passage on the liner *Oriana* for a contingent of Australian surfers to travel to Hawaii with him for the annual Makaha International meet. Among the first to sign up were big-wave chargers Pike and Jackman and 17-year-old Midget Farrelly, who had to borrow half the fare from his boss, board builder Barry Bennett. 'Evo' got enough footage to make his first feature, *Surf Trek to Hawaii*, but it was one of the most miserable winter seasons on record, with frequent rain and unfavourable winds. After weeks of waiting for the Makaha meet to be called on, the Aussies flew home without competing.

Even without proving himself in Hawaii, by the end of 1962 and as Australia's new beach cult exploded in the media, its undisputed poster child was Midget Farrelly. However, Farrelly, although he enjoyed a beer and a laugh as much as the next guy, was nothing like the surfie stereotype in the media. 'They come from good homes, they are well educated. Why, then, do they turn into common larrikins?' one popular magazine asked. Midget could have given them an answer that would have killed their story, but he was on his way back to Hawaii.

Midget was seeded into the Makaha semi-finals as Australian champion, and along with Evans and Dave Jackman arrived to find solid 8-feet sets wrapping around the point. By his own account Midget rode 'well, but not spectacularly', then had to wait until the next day when the finalists were published in the newspaper to find he had made the cut. Again there was a long wait for a new swell and when it came it was marginal, but the event was being filmed for American television for the first time and the producers needed a finish. Thus, on 2 January 1963, the final was on.

Midget cuts back stylishly on the way to winning the first official world championships of surfing, Manly, 1964. Photo Jack Eden.

The finalists – Hawaii's Buffalo Keaulana and Rabbit Kekai, California's Chuck Linden, John Peck and Mike Doyle and Australia's Farrelly – paddled out just after 4 pm. While the other finalists made for the bigger waves on the point, Farrelly went to the more consistent inside waves.

Mike Doyle later wrote: 'An unbelievable thing happened at Makaha that winter. Midget Farrelly, an Australian, only 17 [in fact, Midget had just turned 18] and almost unknown, won . . . Midget was just brilliant. While I rode maybe five outside waves in an hour, Midget rode 30 inside waves, just ripping and tearing . . . He did everything wrong to win, everything against the rules, but it set him apart from the rest of us, and he ended up changing the rules.' Farrelly himself put a peculiar spin on his victory that was to become a familiar refrain: 'I just got sick of the whole thing halfway through and couldn't surf seriously.' Sick of it in his first international event at the age of 18!

None of this mattered back in Australia, where sports-crazed Aussies and their equally sports-crazed media greeted 'Australia's first world surfing champion' with banner headlines and offers of

'He did everything wrong to win, everything against the rules, but it set him apart from the rest of us.'

columns and product endorsements. At the height of the Aussie summer of 1962–63, surfing had blown up as the new teenage rage much as it had in California after the release of the Hollywood film *Gidget* in 1959. And right at the top of the heap was Midget Farrelly.

In the winter of 1962 Midget's friend and mentor Bob Evans started a magazine called *Surfing World*; it soon became known as the 'Midget monthly'. Evo had shot the action at Makaha, which he rush edited and released before the summer was over as the short *Midget Goes Hawaiian*. It was on a double bill with his second full-length feature, *Surfing the Southern Cross*, which also featured Farrelly. The most potent footage from the Makaha event was a shot of Midget walking up the beach after the final, which Evo had cut to the Four Seasons' hit of the moment 'Walk Like a Man'.

If Midget mania went to Farrelly's head, his contemporaries don't remember it. They recall a shy, somewhat awkward young man who

Soul arch at Crescent Head, 1963. Photo Albe Falzon.

frequently seemed embarrassed at the attention he received, but there were subtle signs that fame was beginning to change his once-carefree outlook.

Farrelly's new fame had also turned him into something of a chick magnet. In his middle teens he had dated Tanya Binning, a surfer recognised as being the hottest beach babe of her generation who later found fame in movies. Infatuated, Midget made her a board with 'Tanya' written across the nose, matching his own board with 'Midget' written on it in similar style. However, the love match was by all accounts an innocent one. Now the world champ had the pick of the beach and he chose Pearl Turton, who had just won the women's event at the Australian championships at Avalon.

In the middle of 1963 Midget's father stepped out from behind his taxi during a shift and was knocked down and killed. Apparently overcome with grief, Mrs Farrelly took her own life a week later. Midget never spoke publicly about the impact the double tragedy had on him and his younger sister, then both still teenagers.

By 1963 surfboard riding clubs were peppered up and down Australia's east coast (Midget was founding president of the

The Immortals of Australian Surfing · 12

> Midget never spoke publicly about the impact the double tragedy had on him and his younger sister.

Dee Why club) but no real connection between them and no governing body. In response to this Bob Evans put together a group of prominent surfers that included Midget and formed the founding committee of the Australian Surfriders Association. Midget was elected president, and he nominated his friend and roommate John Witzig as secretary.

While Evans' motives were noble, he did have a secondary agenda. Despite Farrelly's win the previous year, surfers around the world were becoming tired of Makaha's pretensions to being a real world title. They wanted an official world title established, and Evo badly wanted the inaugural championships for Australia. His first move was to enlist major sponsors and stage an Australian invitational surfing championship at Sydney's most popular beach, Bondi, in November 1963, with an airline ticket to Hawaii for the winner. For some reason, perhaps the recent loss of his parents, Midget Farrelly did not compete and the title and ticket went to rising star 'Nat' Young, just a week short of his 16th birthday.

Bondi was a dry run for Evo's main game. As early as February 1963 he had editorialised in *Surfing World*: 'I honestly can't see any obstacle in staging the 1964 World Board Riding Championships in Australia.' And he was right: delighted with the media coverage they had received from Bondi, petroleum company Ampol agreed to be the major sponsor while Australia's national airlines, Qantas and TAA, provided airfares for competitors.

The Ampol World Titles were slated for May at Manly, the beach where Midget Farrelly learned to surf, with Ampol throwing £30,000 (around $1m in today's dollars) at the event and Bob Evans scoring another major coup by having one of Sydney's television stations agree to broadcast the finals live.

The first day of the first official world surfing titles was, in fact, the Australian titles, with the best surfers from Australia's six states vying to compete in the weekend's main event. Midget won it from Mick Dooley and Bobby Brown, and all three were seeded into the quarter finals with the other national champions. An estimated crowd of more than 65,000 turned up at the beach for the Sunday

Midget Farrelly · 13

afternoon finals, while hundreds of thousands more watched it live on black and white television as Hawaiian Joey Cabell and Californians Mike Doyle and L.J. Richards took on the trio of Australians in a one-hour final.

Echoing his sentiments at Makaha, Midget later wrote: 'Right from the start I did not like it. I felt rotten and I did not want to be in it. I just felt so sick of it all . . . I did not feel as though I could be aggressive, and this showed in my riding.'

Photographer Jack Eden recalled: 'Midget had surfed brilliantly in the contest, but not that well in the final . . . but then he got a long-walled wave, walked casually to the nose, trimmed through a soupy section, hung off the tip again, then walked back, put his hands in the air and swung into a beautiful, graceful cutback, setting up for the inside section. I think the hooter sounded halfway through the ride. I knew he'd won.' In fact, Farrelly won by a solid six points, with Doyle and Cabell tied for second. On countback second went to Doyle with Cabell third, Richards fourth, Dooley fifth and Brown sixth. At last it was official: Bernard 'Midget' Farrelly was the world champion.

If Midget mania had been intense after Makaha, after Manly

'I think the hooter sounded halfway through the ride. I knew he'd won.'

it was almost scary. Farrelly's Sunday tabloid column was now syndicated all over Australia and he was frequently seen on TV as the voice of active Australian youth. Introducing one such Midget moment, a presenter on the normally staid *Four Corners* current affairs program said: 'It's taken barely two summers of hard-sell promotion to make the surfboard rival the tennis racquet and the cricket ball as a symbol of Australian sport, and, at the age of 19, Midget Farrelly has become the idol of the blossoming surfie cult.'

Over the summer of 1964–65 and after a short stint with Gordon Woods Surfboards, Midget decided to start producing surfboards under his own name. Assisted by young local surfer Warren Cornish, he set up shop in a boatshed at Palm Beach. The Farrelly boards showed that Midget had learned plenty during his apprenticeship in the surfboard sweatshops of Brookvale: the craftsmanship was exquisite from the beginning. Surfboard guru Bob McTavish said: 'When I first met him

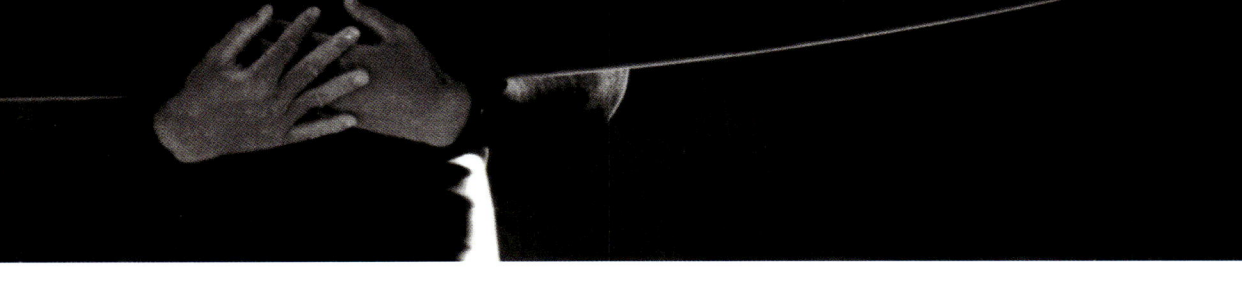

Intense surf check, Palm Beach, 1971. Photo Albe Falzon.

he was still learning his craft, but he was getting a handle on it. In Hawaii in '63 I rode one of his guns and it was magnificent, far more advanced than the Hawaiian boards.'

The 1965 Australian titles were held at Manly in May and featured much the same surf conditions as had the world titles a year earlier. Midget successfully defended his title, but the minor placings revealed a changing cast. Now competing as a senior, Nat Young was a close second while transplanted Queenslander Bob McTavish surfed above himself to finish third. Young's sphinx style of earlier years had evolved into a tight, functional style that extracted maximum control from his huge feet planted on the deck, and both he and McTavish minimised flashy hand gestures. It wasn't much, but keen observers detected the beginning of a new kind of surfing just as they had when Farrelly started nonchalantly throwing his board around in 1961.

Midget returns to competitive surfing, mid-1970s. Photo Jeff Divine.

The rise of Young's star over Farrelly's had become apparent earlier in the year when Young finished second to Felipe Pomar at the second world championships in Peru, while Midget was knocked out in the semi-finals in big, unruly surf. Midget's eight-month reign as official world champion was over. Even the Midget boosters had begun to change teams. Having championed Midget for years, Bob Evans decided to focus on Nat Young for his 1965 film feature *Long Way 'Round*, filming him in Peru and Ecuador surfing, mingling with the aristocracy and generally disporting himself as the Next Big Thing. Years later Farrelly told interviewer Matt Warshaw: 'Everything changed after '64 . . . Australian surfing had been a fairly purist pastime up until that point. But then a fellow called Bob Evans was having as much influence as he could . . . and his importance in the surfing world in large part depended on annually creating new heroes.'

> '**Bernard Farrelly is 21 years old . . . he is not finished, or superseded like last year's model.**'

John Witzig, a good surfer and former roommate of Midget's, while guest editing for the globetrotting Bob Evans devoted the July/August issue of *Surfing World* to the 'new era'. It was hard to avoid such pointed references as the headline 'An End to an Era?' next to a hero shot of Midget with his 1963 Makaha trophy, but Witzig tried to balance the ledger by writing: 'The new era movement appears to be a little out of perspective . . . Bernard Farrelly is 21 years old . . . he is not finished, or superseded like last year's model.'

A few weeks after the magazine's publication Nat Young, riding a thinner and more responsive surfboard than most and displaying a controlled, functional approach to riding in the most critical part of the wave, won the 1966 world championships in San Diego, California. There was no doubt that this was a benchmark, but what we tend to forget is that Farrelly also made the final of this event riding a radical, lightweight, stringerless board that was arguably ahead of Young's in design terms.

In fact, in the revolutionary surfing year of 1967, while McTavish, Young and Californian George Greenough spearheaded the shortboard revolution and got all the column inches, Farrelly was quietly refining his stringerless designs at the Palm Beach boathouse, emerging every week or so to surf Palm Beach or North Avalon on a lighter, shorter, more radical board. Bob McTavish now concedes that competition with Midget hurried the revolution along:

> *People think that he dropped his bundle after the New Era thing, but it was quite the opposite. During that period, when Nat was world champion and spending a lot of time skiing, Midget was a passionate, dedicated surfer and shaper. We were neck and neck from July to November of '67. We'd surf 100 yards apart on the same beach, not wanting the other to see the design refinements we'd made.*

In December 1967 world title finalist Bobby Brown was killed in a pub by a thug with a broken beer glass. It was a tragic loss to surfing, and few felt it more than

Farrelly. Early in 1968 he was the star attraction at a memorial contest held at Sandshoes Reef in Cronulla. Riding a slightly V-bottomed pintail of around 8 feet, he drew classic fast lines across the little waves and won the event at a canter.

Anyone who had not already revised their opinion that Midget was a has-been would surely have done so later that year after he came second at the world titles in November in Puerto Rico. Nat Young came fourth and was hardly out of the picture, but it was Farrelly's down-the-line pintail tracks that created the most attention and he was unlucky not to win a second world title when the judges preferred Fred Hemmings' straight-ahead approach.

During the period between the 1968 world titles and the 1970 world's in Victoria, Australia, Midget Farrelly Surfboards became widely recognised as the Rolls Royces of surfboards in terms of both craftsmanship and progressive design. By then shortboards had become universally accepted, and most of the leading Australian surfers had embraced the logic that shorter was better to an alarming extent. This became apparent when California's Rolf Aurness claimed the 1970 world title by simply riding the right board for the waves. Second placer Farrelly was the only Australian to follow suit, riding a short but sleek pin that gave him speed on the face and down the line.

In 1972 Farrelly established Surfblanks to compete with his old boss Barry Bennett's Dion Chemicals in the foam blank business. He hired 1964 world title finalist Mick Dooley to manage the business, while Midget Farrelly Surfboards, which had been in financial difficulties, retreated to a secret shaping bay and glassing room hidden under the garage of a rambling house the Farrellys had bought at Palm Beach, overlooking the broad expanse of Pittwater. Asked to comment years later about their working relationship, loyal friend Mick Dooley said of his mate Bernie:

> *We have surfed, competed, sailed, and worked together. He even tried to teach me to hang glide. He is a good family man with a loving wife, a younger sister, three daughters, son in-laws [sic] and grandchildren. He is what some people might call a perfectionist. Can be difficult to be around sometimes, but worth it. I have found him to be a generous person, giving of his time and knowledge, if you were willing to listen,*

Portrait by Ron Stoner, late 1960s.

> *especially of surfing and surfboard manufacturing . . . When we were in our teens and early twenties he was without a doubt the very best surfer in Australia. Full of fun, always looking to jump in the car and go on a surf trip to some new surf spot. They were the days. Great memories.*

After his disappointing second in the 1970 world titles, Farrelly won the Gunston 500 in South Africa. When the pro tour arrived in Australia a few years later he finished fourth in the inaugural Rip Curl Pro at Bells Beach in 1973. Not yet 30, he was far from a spent force but he never competed at the top level again, preferring to devote his time to his family, businesses and passion for the gliding sports in water and on air. In 1985 he was inducted into the Sports Australia Hall of Fame.

When the longboard started to make its dramatic return to favour in the 1990s Midget Farrelly was a popular drawcard at several events, surfing with ageless grace in the legends exhibitions alongside his contemporaries – with one notable exception. He always made it a condition of his appearance that Nat Young would not be there. Such was the case when a re-enactment of the 1964 world title final was conducted at the Noosa Festival of Surfing in 1999. The standard of surfing in the exhibition was remarkable from all five living finalists, but the big crowd on the beach had Midget as the clear-cut winner.

Farrelly continued to ride his own boards and body surf well through his 60s and beyond along Sydney's Northern Beaches, on occasional sorties up the coast and on Tavarua, Fiji. Diagnosed with stomach cancer in 2012, he continued to build surfboards and ride them whenever his health allowed and rode his final waves with his family at his beloved Tavarua just days before the disease claimed him. He died in Sydney on 7 August 2016.

Midget Farrelly · 19

Nat Young on his way to winning the world title in San Diego, 1966. Photo Ron Stoner.

2

NAT YOUNG

Full name	Robert Harold Young
Nickname	The Gnat, Nat
Birthdate	14 November 1947
Place of birth	Sydney, New South Wales

Known as 'The Animal' in his glory years, Nat Young brought a muscular new approach to surfing by riding the wave rather than the surfboard.

Although he had to play second fiddle to Midget Farrelly at the dawn of the surf boom in Australia in the early 1960s, Robert 'Nat' Young was never going to accept that role for long and he didn't, soon eclipsing his then friend and mentor.

By 1966 Young had become Australia's second world champion and a legendary, if somewhat polarising, figure in world surfing. He led the way into a new approach to surfing that was often described as 'riding the wave' as opposed to 'riding the surfboard'. Tall and gangly with huge feet, he combined great power with perfect timing and an elegant style as he manoeuvred the heavy longboards of the time closer to the curl of the wave than anyone had ridden before.

While his aggressive demeanour in the surf sometimes made him enemies, few baby boomer surfers would deny that Nat, like Midget before him, was the greatest single influence on how the art of riding a wave was approached. And, as someone once tagged a toilet wall on Sydney's Northern Beaches, 'Nat's Nat and that's that!'

Born in Sydney's Western Suburbs in 1947, Robert Young became 'The Gnat' when he started surfing in the late 1950s, soon after the family had moved from land-bound suburbia to Collaroy on the Northern Beaches. He was so named for a puny frame that looked

Fifteen-year-old Nat Young after winning his first major event, the Australian Invitational, Bondi, 1963. Photo John Witzig.

rather awkward and inconsequential as he attempted to guide his first giant (10'6"/315 cm) balsa board – christened the 'Queen Mary' by its previous owner after what was then the largest ship afloat – across the gentle shore break in front of the family home.

He may have looked like an insect on an ocean liner in 1957, but how deceptive beginnings can be. By the early 1960s Nat Young had grown into his body and become the fastest-rising young star on Sydney's beaches, heavily influenced by his idol, Midget Farrelly. Just three years older, Midget was already regarded as Australia's best surfer and, mature beyond his years, he became Nat's first mentor and travel companion on numerous surf trips up and down the coast. This in turn led to Nat being introduced to the social circle of surfing film-maker and entrepreneur Bob Evans, one of the most influential figures in the emerging sport.

Evans had been a keen surfer and surf lifesaver since the late 1940s despite being forced to wear a colostomy bag from a very early age following surgery for bowel cancer. In 1956 he had been part of a group of Sydney surfers who watched an exhibition staged at Avalon Beach by visiting Californian and Hawaiian lifeguards of a surfboard known as the Malibu Chip. Unlike the hollow plywood, 16-feet (480 cm) Australian boards known as 'toothpicks', Malibu Chips were only 10 feet (3 m) long and were built of lightweight balsa, and they featured a tailfin that enabled them to be turned along a wave face. This was a game changer for surfing in Australia, and Bob Evans had bought one before the lifeguards left the country.

Ahead of the curve in seeing how the surf craze might take off, Evans made the bold decision to focus not on manufacturing surfboards like several of his friends but on stoking the fire by screening surf documentaries up and down the coast, starting with American imports but soon producing his own – doing everything himself from filming the action to manning the projector. He soon added a magazine, *Surfing World*, to his growing surf media business.

> He may have looked like an insect on an ocean liner in 1957, but how deceptive beginnings can be.

An Evans movie roadshow along the coast was an opportunity to shoot photos for the magazine and film action sequences for his next release, so he took along the best young surfers he could find. Schoolkid Nat Young was initially very much a second stringer in the Evans camp, particularly after Farrelly won the unofficial world championships at Makaha in Hawaii in January 1963, documented by Evans in his second film *Midget Goes Hawaiian*. However, the second-fiddle connection brought Nat closer to Midget. As early as 1961 Nat was part of a group that included Midget on a road trip to Queensland, but two years later he found himself

Nat with the world championship trophy, 1966. Photo Ron Stoner.

accompanying the unofficial world champion to Bells Beach, Victoria for the Easter board rally.

As Young wrote in his autobiography:

'I can remember feeling so proud sitting up like Jackie in the front seat of Midget's brand new 179 Holden station wagon as we accelerated out of Sydney on our way to the second [annual] contest at Bells Beach . . . He was my absolute hero, and here I was, sitting in his 179 looking up at our two boards strapped side by side on the roof rack.'

After the Bells trip Midget and Nat partnered for several promotions, including a surfing exhibition in Newcastle, after which they were taken to a menswear store and told they could choose some clothing. Nat later wrote:

I'd already been given a cheque for twenty five pounds in payment for the exhibition – I couldn't believe my luck . . . I really needed a suit. I just knew it was the next step towards becoming a professional surfer, although there was no such thing at the time . . .

The store gave me a nice blue suit, which I treasured for years. I wore it when Bob Evans, Midget and I met the Lord Mayor of Sydney [at a reception] before I left on my first overseas trip.

That trip – to Hawaii – was the prize Nat had won, aged just a week short of 16, when he took out the open division of the Australian invitational championship at Bondi, a contest Midget had declined to enter. It was by no means a changing of the guard and even less so when Midget won the first official world surfing championships six months later, which had been organised by Bob Evans and held at Manly in May 1964. That ground-breaking event, in which Nat finished second in the junior division, propelled Midget Farrelly into the limelight in a way no Australian surfboard rider had previously been. Suddenly he was a teenage idol who was almost singlehandedly responsible for igniting the surf craze.

Strangely, during 1964 Evans began to shift his allegiance from the champion to the challenger, perhaps in determination to again stay ahead of the curve. Nat wrote in his autobiography: 'Looking through [mother] Greta's scrapbook,

I counted nineteen trips to the north coast with Evo in 1964. Lots of time spent together in the car provided the perfect opportunity for lots of talk about just about everything.'

At first much of what they talked about was Nat's increasingly difficult home life, in which he was in frequent conflict with his domineering father Harold. Evans, who had three children of his own, offered wise counsel in a role that Nat later referred to as 'my dad in all but name'. Throughout 1964 and 1965 Evans also tutored Nat in the finer points of being a champion, such as knowing how to navigate a wine list, make an acceptance speech and dress appropriately. Nat was a fast learner. Evans was at his side with the cameras rolling for his next film, *Long Way Round*, when Young finished second in challenging waves in the second world titles in Peru in 1965, and it seemed only a matter of time before the charismatic teenager would be recognised as being the best.

Midget Farrelly, who had also flown to Peru with Evans and Nat, had been eliminated in the semi-finals, although he fared better in the small-wave specialty event. Even though he remained near the top of world surfing for many of the following years, Midget had begun to feel threatened by the rising star of his protégé and distanced himself from Evans while sowing the seeds with Nat of what would become Australian surfing's most bitter and long-standing feud.

Nat's surfing was fast and aggressive but still slightly derivative of his early influences, including Farrelly and Californian Phil Edwards. Then, in 1965, he hooked up with surfer/shaper Bob McTavish, a design visionary who was pioneering a new, functional approach to surfing in the small but perfect waves of Noosa Heads while shaping boards for Hayden Kenny Surfboards at Alexandra Headland, just down the coast. Using Noosa as his training ground through the winter of 1965, Nat soon became the best exponent of the new style of wave riding that concentrated on staying close to the curl of the breaking wave.

He later wrote of his first experience of Noosa's Tea Tree Bay:

> *Those first few waves are etched in my mind. In surf like this I could be so much more accurate than in the Sydney beach break. The take-off exploded in the same spot every time, perfect for*

Nat testing the new vee bottom designs at big Honolua Bay, 1967. Photo John Witzig.

> *a classic Phil Edwards top turn, then into a long-running wall . . . My board was giving me a bit of trouble because it was designed for Sydney's small, gutless beach breaks . . . it dawned on me what McTavish had been saying . . . about thinner boards and finer rails.*

Before he returned to Queensland for more training sessions at Noosa and for the Australian championships at Coolangatta in the late autumn of 1966, Nat designed and shaped a McTavish-influenced, lighter, thin-railed surfboard at the Gordon Woods factory in Sydney and then won the New South Wales titles and the Bells Beach Easter Classic on it. It was a magic board. He christened it 'Sam', and back in Queensland's thin and fast point-break waves he comprehensively won the Australian titles and then fine-tuned his partnership with the board at Noosa.

Seemingly now unstoppable, Nat took Sam to the 1966 world titles in San Diego, California with high hopes that together they would bring home another world title for Australia. However, American surfing had become obsessed with one element of riding the longboards of the day. Nose riding, or dangling five or 10 toes over the nose of the board while riding through falling sections, was often beautiful to watch but also extremely difficult.

To Australian eyes, nose riding was part of the performance and not the whole deal. To American eyes, there was only one way the San Diego world titles could go. Hawaiian-born California resident David Nuuhiwa, a tall, charismatic surfer with a long mane of black hair and a cat-like style as he walked the board, had become the undisputed king of nose riding and was considered by most

Nat in control at Haleiwa, 1968. Photo Ron Stoner.

American surfers to be the world champion in waiting. Nat Young had other ideas, and after a week spent acclimatising to Californian conditions in Santa Barbara he and his small entourage – which included his friend, surf journalist John Witzig, who had recently chronicled Nat's ascension in the controversial new era edition of *Surfing World* – drove south to San Diego.

San Diego 1966 turned out to be the last world titles surfed on longboards, just ahead of an equipment revolution led by Bob McTavish in Australia and Dick Brewer in Hawaii that saw the length of most surfboards drop by as much as a metre. But the defining difference between Young and Nuuhiwa, not to mention most of the other American competitors, was that Nat was already bringing shortboard sensibilities to his surfing. While he still embodied the style and grace of traditional surfing, he was able to snap directional changes on Sam's egg-shaped rails and carve deeper lines out of his bottom turns. In less than ideal conditions, the Australian flicked his board around the curl and introduced a new dynamic to the sport.

To Australian eyes, nose riding was part of the performance and not the whole deal.

As Bob McTavish's number-one test pilot Young also played a part in the subsequent development of the shortboard in Australia over the ensuing years, but the broad acceptance of the idea that surfing was about riding the wave rather than the board dates back to Nat Young's stellar San Diego performance.

Although Nuuhiwa didn't make it to the podium in San Diego, Nat regarded him as his only real threat in the competition. After the event the two rivals became friends, speeding off for a celebratory weekend in Las Vegas in Nat's brand new gold Chevrolet Camaro, his prize for winning the title. For Nat, who was about to turn 19, this was his real introduction to the high life, a life he had caught glimpses of at expensive club lunches in Sydney with Bob Evans and at the exclusive Club Waikiki in Peru. Now he was the world champion, and suddenly there were no boundaries.

While Midget Farrelly had become a household name in Australia after his victories in 1963 and 1964, Nat Young's elevation to superstar in 1966 has to be seen in a different context. The first great surf craze had finished, and although Young's dominant alpha personality and good looks made him regular fodder for the social as well as the sports pages, his primary influence was felt within surfing itself. There it was huge: not only was he considered to be the most technically advanced surfer in the world, but he was also developing the template for a professional surfer.

Winning a flashy sports car didn't make you a professional, and in surfing substantial cash purses were almost a decade away, but Nat was suddenly in demand from media organisations and, more importantly, from commercial sponsors. Within weeks of winning the world title he had secured lucrative deals with White Stag wetsuits, Speedo swimwear and Dewey Weber Surfboards, probably the biggest board manufacturer in the US at the time.

The art of the deal was something Nat had quickly picked up from Bob Evans and from cricketing great Richie Benaud, whose sports representation agency had helped set him up very early in his career. Nat may not have finished

Nat was suddenly in demand from media organisations and, more importantly, from commercial sponsors.

school, but he knew how to work a boardroom back in the days when most surfers thought that was the place you put your surfboards. Consequently, Nat was rarely without sponsorships and marketing deals.

Although his post–world title competitive record suffers somewhat by comparison with Midget Farrelly's he was still considered the gold standard of surfing, not just in Australia but around the world. From 1966 until well into the 70s he maintained his edge better than all of his contemporaries – although Midget was close – as surfboards transitioned from long to short. His powerful yet elegant style on both influenced an entire generation of surfers, while his positioning of himself as an elder statesman of the sport and culture guaranteed he remained at the forefront even when flirtations with the drug culture in the early 1970s brought him the wrong kind of headlines.

In 1969 Nat moved into the stunning house he'd had built at

The Immortals of Australian Surfing · 30

Young was the gold standard in an era when surfboards transitioned from long to short. Photo Ron Stoner.

Whale Beach with his school-days sweetheart Marilyn Bennett, whom he had married earlier that year. It was a beautiful place with panoramic ocean views, but somehow Nat was still restless. The following year, after driving to the Queensland Gold Coast for the Australian championships, he and Marilyn stopped off at Byron Bay for a few days and fell in love with what Byron had become: the centre of surfing's new country soul culture. On the spot they bought an old house on acreage and with views of the surf breaks, and within a few months they had rented out Whale Beach and moved north.

The move to the country changed Nat's approach to surfing and life in general, but the arrival of professional surfing contests over the next few years interrupted his hippie reverie. Invited to surf in the first

Young competing in the longboard division of the Rip Curl Pro France in the early 1990s. Photo Joli.

Surfabout event in Sydney in May 1974, which was hyped as offering the world's richest prize money, Nat's aggressive approach to riding waves returned and he finished in third place behind new sensation Michael Peterson, who had modelled his approach on Nat's.

Never one to let a promotional opportunity slip by, Nat stunned the awards ceremony when he donated his $600 prize money to the Labor Party's re-election fund. A few days later he found himself sitting next to besieged prime minister Gough Whitlam at the campaign launch. Although this skirmish may have given Nat a taste for politics, it was more than a decade before he threw his own hat in the ring and ran on environmental issues as an independent candidate for the New South Wales seat of Pittwater, mostly at the urging of his friend, Midnight Oil frontman Peter Garrett. It was a safe Liberal seat and Nat was never expected to win but the closeness of the result frightened the life out of Nat, who suddenly saw himself sitting in parliament while the surf was pumping. It was not to be.

Divorced from Marilyn and remarried to Ti Deaton, Nat reinvented himself as a surfer in

> **Picking up where he'd left off in 1966, Nat won four world longboard titles between 1986 and 1990.**

the 1980s when the ageing surfer demographic made longboarding a popular subset of the sport. Picking up where he'd left off in 1966, Nat won four world longboard titles between 1986 and 1990. Well into his 40s, he also found himself sponsored by international companies again as well as modelling for Ralph Lauren and featuring on the cover of *Vogue*.

To say it has been a well-rounded and adventurous life is to understate it: now well into his 70s, Nat Young is still surfing with power and style on both shortboard and longboard, and he remains one of surfing's most enduring figures.

Lynch comes off the top during the Mundaka swell event of 1989. Photo Joli.

WAYNE LYNCH

Full name	Wayne Lynch
Nickname	The Fish
Birthdate	15 January 1952
Place of birth	Colac, Victoria

Still one of Australia's most revered surfer/shapers, Wayne Lynch has spent a lifetime trying to surf under the radar.

Wayne Lynch is not the only surfer whose destiny was shaped by becoming a child prodigy, but in Australia he was probably our first.

Lynch was born the son of a fisherman in the timber town of Colac in western Victoria in 1952, and his formative years were spent as a water baby in the seaside resort town of Lorne. His first surfing influence was family friend Gail Couper, five years his senior and destined to become a legend of women's surfing. Although they started surfing at roughly the same time riding balsa Malibu surfboards on the protected waves of Lorne Point, she provided the early lead in pushing the younger boy to improve. Under Gail's early influence Wayne showed a natural talent by the age of 10, and a year later he won his first contest at Phillip Island when aged just 11.

Although the results weren't challenged, having the youngest competitor win an open event was considered an embarrassment by the organisers, who gave him a wave of the day award instead of the trophy. In later years this resulted in Lynch often contending that contest results were an inexact science. Over time this throwaway line would become a mantra for Lynch and an army of acolytes that followed his path away from the competitive arena to the more rarified air of soul or spiritual surfing, over which he arguably had the most profound influence in Australian surfing history. But this was all for the future: in the 1960s the talented young goofy footer's eyes were on the prize, and he quickly became the poster child for the sport.

Still only 13, Lynch won the first of six consecutive Victorian junior titles in 1965 and was soon a standout performer backside at Bells Beach on bigger days, his delicate, precise style disguising the power of his turns. In the autumn of 1966 his mother May chaperoned him to the Queensland Gold Coast for his first Australian titles, and although he missed out on taking out the juniors division, his complete and mature backhand approach on right-hand point waves in difficult conditions attracted the attention of older competitors and the surf media.

Surfing World photojournalist John Witzig blew up a photo of the young teenager performing a radical vertical manoeuvre on a big board and captioned it 'Is this the future world champion?' Witzig titled an accompanying brief interview 'What is there interesting about a 14-year-old kid from Lorne called Wayne Lynch?', but he already knew. Decades later Lynch told writer Sean Doherty:

> *I used to have dreams about surfing. I'd be watching people surf in my dreams. Just as I was falling asleep there's a point where you're not awake and you're not asleep, and I'd have these images of people surfing in my head and they'd be doing these amazing things off the lip – what we call today re-entries – and they'd do 360 degree turns, and it was all really fluid and I saw it in my mind and I went, maybe this is possible.*

Back home in Victoria, the goofy-footed *wunderkind* soon came to the attention of more senior surfers. Footballer and big-wave rider John Monie befriended him at the Bells Beach event and took Lynch off on early surf trips to New South Wales and South Australia, and Lynch's maths teacher at Lorne High School, Brian Singer, surfed with him before and after school. Later, when Singer founded Rip Curl with Doug Warbrick, Wayne Lynch was one of the brand's first team riders and quickly became its leading advertising asset.

Having failed to win the national junior title on his first attempt, Lynch won it four consecutive times. He started with the 1967 event

Lynch in his prime, Airey's Inlet, 1975. Photo Stephen Cooney.

held close to home at Bells Beach, where again his backhand surfing on waves of consequence impressed the elders of Australian surfing. In the same year Lynch started shaping his own surfboards in the workshop his father Bill, who had become a builder when fishing got too tough, had created on the family property near Lorne. As Lynch told Sean Doherty: 'Dad was a good builder, very thorough. So I guess I probably inherited some feeling for things like that, although I was not very talented at shaping at all.'

Maybe not but he was a fast learner, and the third board he shaped turned out to be magic. As Lynch said:

Thirteen-year-old prodigy Wayne Lynch sits with veteran Snow McAllister, waiting for his heat at the Newcastle Mattara contest, 1965. Photo Surfing Australia.

It had the wide point back of centre and had a rounded tail. There were boards back in the early years called 'teardrops'. Very pointed at the front, they looked just like a water droplet. All the width and all the curve was in the tail. I had a mate who would come down to Lorne in the holidays and he had a teardrop and I was astounded at how much better that board felt than my old balsa mal. When I started shaping my own boards I never forgot the freedom that board had and the way you could roll into direction changes. The transition from one turn to another was very fluid, and the front, because it was narrow, was light to turn.

When I shaped that board I had no set theory at all, and over the years I've gone back to shaping like this, on instinct more than anything. I was so young, 15, and I had no reason behind what I was doing, it was just what I felt. But the thing was phenomenal. What I didn't understand then, and what was key with those boards along with the weight and flex, was the end curve. So that board started to let me surf a different way, the way I wanted to, trying new things.

Lynch's rudimentary design innovations came at a time when what would become known as the shortboard evolution was taking off in Australia and Hawaii. Creative wizards such as shaper Bob McTavish experimented with shorter and shorter surfboards in the quest for greater manoeuvrability, initially cutting a foot or more off the nose of the old longboards and reshaping them. By the end of 1967 the shortboard revolution had taken hold, with test pilots such as Nat Young riding the wide-tail McTavish boards and Midget Farrelly taking a more moderate line with his smaller stringerless models.

What distinguished Lynch's emerging teardrop designs were the tracks the boards enabled him to take on a wave, and there was no doubting that his vertical tracks on a wave were at the cutting edge of performance surfing. As Sean Doherty put it: 'It wasn't the fact that he was winning, it was how he was winning. On purpose-shaped boards, he'd jam a bottom turn, bury half his board, and train it straight at the lip.'

John Witzig had seen this coming, and by 1968 he wasn't alone among Australia's more astute observers of surfing. However, it wasn't until his film-maker brother Paul became involved that Wayne Lynch exploded on the world stage. Paul Witzig got his start in surf films shooting sequences for Bruce Brown's ground-breaking *The Endless Summer* in the early 1960s, and subsequently produced his own first feature, *A Life in the Sun*, in 1966. He followed it with *The Hot Generation*, which was released in 1968.

By that time Paul had developed a vision for the future of the surf film genre – dynamic action, driving rock soundtrack, no narration divulging the secret spots being surfed – that was to become standard in the 1970s, and he decided to trial it by emulating Bruce Brown and travelling the world to surf new or little-known breaks. He chose Europe as his main focus and for his cast of surfers Nat Young, 1966 world champion and the biggest name in the sport at the time, rising Sydney stylist Ted Spencer and 15-year-old Wayne Lynch.

Witzig and his cast travelled the Atlantic coast from France to Morocco, where they filmed the Australians creating new tracks on

> **'A boy wonder with searing eyes, a disarming choirboy smile, and an attacking style that often left him upside-down in the curl.'**

previously unknown waves. Wherever they went in Europe they were fêted, and it proved to be a huge awakening for the teenager from small-town Victoria. On the way home the group travelled via Puerto Rico for the 1968 world championships, where defending champion Young lost his crown and Lynch, competing in the open division and internationally for only the second time (he had beaten Young to win the European championships in France a couple of months earlier), was deemed the most progressive surfer in the event, although poor wave selection saw him eliminated in the semi-finals. 'He was the future of surfing incarnate,' Hawaiian surfer Reno Abellira, who also went close to winning, said of Lynch. 'A boy wonder with searing eyes, a disarming choirboy smile, and an attacking style that often left him upside-down in the curl, only to recover in mid-air and land back on his wax.'

The Immortals of Australian Surfing · 40

A young Wayne on an early Evolution board, Palm Beach, 1968. Photo John Pennings.

For Lynch and his new friend Nat Young, the losses in Puerto Rico didn't matter: they believed they were on the edge of taking performance surfing into a new realm.

Witzig's film, aptly titled *Evolution*, was released in 1969, and while some of the reviews were lukewarm it moved quickly from cult favourite to worldwide hit. 'It captured the spirit of the times,' surf historian Matt Warshaw wrote, 'for the most part a showcase for Wayne Lynch, the 17-year-old surfing sensation from Victoria.' (In fact, Lynch was still 16 when the film premiered.) *Evolution* had its Australian premiere at Sydney's Union Theatre, with leading acid-rock band Tamam Shud playing their soundtrack songs live from the orchestra pit. The superimposed images of surfers on waves, an idea borrowed from the underground film genre, heightened an atmosphere that some described as 'euphoric'.

This was nothing when compared with the American premiere at the Hoover Auditorium in San Diego, recalled by film-maker Alan Rich for film historian Albie Thoms in his book *Surfmovies*: 'The opening images of Wayne Lynch had the audience hooting and hollering so

Wayne at home in Victoria with his Rip Curl quiver, 1975. Photo Stephen Cooney.

loudly that the first 15 minutes of the soundtrack was drowned out.' Overnight, Wayne Lynch became a superstar in surfing's biggest marketplace.

In closing the chapter he titled 'Evolution', Albie Thoms noted that the film marked the end of the shortboard revolution and the beginning of the 'era of soul-surfing'. It was a prescient remark, because many in the Australian surfing community, Lynch included, were starting to embrace a simpler lifestyle with surfing for surfing's sake at its core. He competed in the Australian titles at Margaret River, Western Australia and the Bells Beach Classic in 1969, winning the junior divisions in both, but then began to distance himself from competitive surfing and his newfound superstardom. He told Sean Doherty:

> It came back to how I was [being] mythologised in surfing . . . I didn't want to live that life. I loved my life as it was; I just loved it. I grew up in a remarkably beautiful place and I had friends who were very similarly minded, and I went out into the big world of surfing and all the intrigue and the politics and the rivalries, and I was just a kid. And the

attention started to be a little too much and I was expected to do amazing things every time I was in the water. I started to feel the pressure and I started to lose the joy of going surfing, of just being a kid and experimenting . . .

I was a victim of my own creation. And I wasn't going to do that. I wasn't going to go out and do 10 re-entries for the rest of my life to please other people. I just went, these bastards are mad! I don't want any part of this; I'm going home! And I was so stoked to get home 'cause there was none of that where I grew up; it didn't exist. We all shared the surfing and we were overjoyed. It was the best thing we'd ever found. Those aspects of discovery: from surf breaks to what's possible within yourself as a surfer, developing as a person because you're developing your own physical and mental strength, surfing gives you so much. I just saw the rest of it as a distraction.

While it's worth noting that Lynch emerged from obscurity for long enough to travel to Queensland in 1970 and win his last national junior title, for the most part he remained underground over the next couple of years, particularly so after he was conscripted for national service in 1972. He said he never saw his draft papers because his mother, a passionate advocate for social justice, did not want him to be forced to fight in the Vietnam War. In fact, Vietnam service for conscripts was made voluntary in 1971, but the die was cast for Lynch and he lived in his car or in rough bush camps to avoid detection until the new Whitlam Labor government abolished conscription at the end of 1972.

During this period Lynch said he reconnected with Aboriginal lore and practices that his mother had taught him as a child, and his deep respect for First Nations peoples has remained with him. He declined to speak about his actual time spent as an outlaw or reveal where he hid out for many years, but he told Sean Doherty: 'I've had some fairly odd things said to me in recent years . . . I was against the war, and if people don't go, there's no war. That's the reality. But a lot of people went because they had no choice or they didn't understand what they were being sent into . . . I was never against the people who went. I had friends who went to Vietnam, friends whose lives were ruined by it.'

With the conscription monkey off his back, Lynch re-emerged blinking into the sunlight of his fame to discover that a funny thing had happened: in his absence, his legend had grown. In mid-1973 he was invited to travel to Bali with film-maker David 'Mexican' Sumpter. He recalled: 'I remember the year before [while still in hiding] sneaking into a theatre so no one would recognise me to watch *Morning of the Earth* and I loved the film . . . It was very inspiring to me while I was on the run, but it also inspired me to go to Bali as soon as I was able to. Suddenly I'm in Bali with all these lefts, and it was a great trip. I went back soon after and had some amazing surf, but I had a motorbike accident.'

Although he suffered a broken collarbone and a sprained back, Lynch later said that he stayed in the hospital in Bali longer than he needed to so he could support his girlfriend, who had suffered severe facial injuries. While there he contracted malaria and developed complications. Back in Australia he continued to shed weight while doctors tried to determine whether there was something else wrong with him. He was unable to surf for more than a year, and while he

> **Lynch re-emerged blinking into the sunlight of his fame to discover that a funny thing had happened: in his absence, his legend had grown.**

said some had written him off as a surfing force, for the majority his return in 1974 was heralded as a resurrection.

Though adulation for him had not diminished, the surfing world around Lynch had begun a fundamental change. By 1973 three Australian surf brands had emerged that would eventually become the global leaders of a multi–billion dollar industry: Rip Curl, Quiksilver and Billabong. These three funded the growth of professional surfing in Australia and later around the world, starting with the 1973 Rip Curl Bells Beach Pro.

Rip Curl and Quiksilver, which had both grown out of Lynch's own local surfing community on what is now known as the 'Surf Coast', were founded by Lynch's surfing buddies. He was sponsored by Rip Curl at various times and also had his own commercial surfboard brand in the wake of the *Evolution* success, but the reluctant surf star felt uneasy about commercialisation. Years later he told an interviewer: 'In the '60s and '70s there were very vital conversations in the surf community about the environment and society. We were redefining, in many ways, what it meant to be a human on this planet. Somehow those conversations got marginalized and were forgotten. Surfing became more about marketing a product, and a lot of the people inside the industry didn't care.'

In 1974 the addition of the Coca Cola/2SM Surfabout to the Bells Classic made the Australian pro tour the richest in the world and the following year, returning to health and overcoming his misgivings, Lynch went pro. What he immediately found was that while the money was good, there was a lot of competition for it. In his absence a new breed of hungry young pro surfers had emerged, led by Queensland's Michael Peterson.

Wayne at home among the gum trees: Wreck Bay, 1992. Photo Joli.

Lynch at Mundaka, Spain, 1989. Photo Joli.

If there had been an official surfing world tour in 1974, Peterson would have been its champion. In 1975 he hit the ground running, taking out the Bells Beach Pro (Lynch finished sixth) and going into the Surfabout in Sydney as hot favourite.

Lynch later said of Peterson that he was the second most competitive surfer he'd ever come across after Nat Young, but the two were like chalk and cheese. Whereas Lynch's radical manoeuvres were linked with smooth, flowing turns, Peterson was all hand jive and manic force on the wave. In the parlance of the vinyl records of the day, one was on 33 rpm and the other on 78. Surfing beautifully from heats to final, Wayne Lynch took out his first professional victory, which came with a prize cheque of $3,500 – enough for him to re-establish his surfboard business and join the emerging pro tour when it suited him.

After competing in several events in 1976 Lynch finished 11th in the inaugural International Professional Surfers world tour, went AWOL in 1977 and returned in 1978 to finish second at the Surfabout in a nail-biter final in near perfect waves and second at the Katin Pro-Am in California. He then retired again.

Although Lynch donned the competitor's jersey a couple more

Over the past 20 years Wayne Lynch has become one of surfing's strongest environmental advocates, pushing for a more sustainable surfboard industry.

times in the late 1990s for the World Masters Surfing Championships, finishing ninth in Fiji in 1997 and fifth in France in 1999, by that time he had established himself not only as a revered surfer but as one of the most respected surfboard designers and shapers in the world. This accolade hasn't stopped him characteristically taking the odd swipe at his own legend. At a charity surfboard auction in Noosa Heads some years ago he was asked to describe one of his early models, which was about to go under the hammer. 'It was a piece of shit when I made it and it's a piece of shit now,' he declared, leaving the auctioneer wondering where to go next.

Over the past 20 years Wayne Lynch has become one of surfing's strongest environmental advocates, pushing for a more sustainable surfboard industry. as well as supporting many other worldwide causes.

Trademark MP power turn off the bottom at Kirra. Photo dickhoole.com.au.

MICHAEL PETERSON

Full name	Michael Patrick Philp
Nickname	MP, Reg, The Monk
Birthdate	24 September 1952; died 29 March 2012
Place of birth	Brisbane, Queensland

At the top of his sport for a mere handful of years, Michael Peterson left an indelible imprint on surfing.

Although he never won a world title and spent only a handful of short years at the top of his sport, Michael Peterson is unique among the surfing immortals profiled in this book. There has literally never been a surfer like him, and there is never likely to be one.

Apart from his extraordinary natural skills on a surfboard, his audacious competitive spirit and his unbridled gamesmanship, Peterson reached the vortex of his chosen sport because of, not in spite of, the strange and frequently unreachable world he inhabited almost all of his life. Although he couldn't or wouldn't focus on much else for very long, every moment he spent in the competitor's jersey he was 100 per cent focused on winning.

The true facts of his birth only emerged long after the end of his professional surfing career: long after the drug busts, crazy car chases, prison time and residence in psychiatric wards and only as an overweight, middle-aged man in the care of Joan, his loving mum. He was a man whose daily ritual was sitting on a park bench overlooking the ocean, the canvas for his best work, while he sucked on an iced treat like a contented child. Only then could Joan reveal the dark secret that had been her ball and chain for half a century, which she did to her son's biographer Sean Doherty.

Michael Patrick Philp was born during a raging thunderstorm in Brisbane on 24 September 1952, having been conceived after Joan Philp was dragged into a Fortitude Valley boarding house and pack raped by three men while walking home following her barmaid shift. Estranged from her alcoholic mother, Joan spent her pregnancy in a Catholic refuge, working for her keep in a steam laundry before giving birth to a big healthy baby after a difficult three-day labour. A few months after the birth Joan met circus worker Sid 'Peanuts' Peterson, and when she fell pregnant with Michael's brother Tom it was decided that the children should take the Peterson name. On the night in February 1954 when Joan went into labour she was living in a one-room shack on the Tweed River that was ravaged by floodwaters and she had to be rowed across the swollen river to a waiting ambulance. When Tommy was born Sid deserted Joan for the first of many times.

One son born in a thunderstorm, one born in flood: if there was some kind of symbolism in this it was too early to tell. It's also too easy to imagine that, coming from a long line of losers, Michael was born with

> One son born in a thunderstorm, one born in flood: if there was some kind of symbolism in this it was too early to tell.

a passion to change the course of genetics and become a winner, but Michael's genetics were unknown and Joan Philp was and remains in her 90s anything but a loser. She is a warm, strong-willed woman who was a rock for her champion son as his life drifted down paths none could have imagined.

The traumatic circumstances of Michael's birth may well account for some of the difficulties he later experienced, but Joan's strength kept the family together through the tough times living in various houses in the struggle-street section of Tweed Heads South, right on the Queensland/New South Wales border. By the early 1960s Michael was a Nipper champion at Greenmount Surf Club, already standing up on rubber Surfoplanes and coolite boards. He soon moved onto real surfboards and by his early teens was regarded as the hottest young surfer in the Coolangatta/Kirra area, a gangly, awkward figure on the beach who miraculously

Picking up the winner's trophy was like second nature to MP, Queensland titles, 1975. Photo Surfing Queensland, courtesy Richard Harvey.

transformed into a slick speed machine the moment he stood on a surfboard. Wayne 'Rabbit' Bartholomew and Peter Townend, a year or two younger, were right up there as well along with goofy footer Andrew McKinnon, but Michael had a scarily intense desire to be better than the rest and particularly after he got onto a shortboard early in 1968.

That was the year pioneer surfboard shaper Joe Larkin, a Sydney transplant, took both Peterson and Townend under his wing and taught them the rudiments of shaping. In 1969 he included Peterson in an older group of local surfers he drove across the country to compete in the Australian titles at Margaret River, Western Australia, Peterson having just qualified by virtue of a third-place finish in the Queensland juniors. At Margaret's Wayne Lynch more than had Peterson's measure, but Peterson's loose-limbed, frenetic surfing style impressed some of the talent scouts. His special talents were becoming well known, although he had yet to make a serious breakthrough as the 1970 season began. He was determined that this would be his

Michael Peterson · 51

And the winner is . . . Mark Richards masks his disappointment as MP wins the inaugural Stubbies Pro, Burleigh Heads, 1977. Photo Dan Merkel.

year but in the junior division of the Queensland titles he could only manage third again, this time behind McKinnon and Townend.

As Easter approached Joe Larkin again loaded up his van with young surfers and headed south to Bells Beach, where Peterson would go head to head against Wayne Lynch in his last season as a junior. Looking for revenge for his hiding at Margaret River the previous year, in clean, small conditions Peterson seemed to grow in confidence with each round before dispatching Lynch in the semi-finals and going on to win the final from Andrew McKinnon and Sydney's Grant Oliver.

The young Queenslander was ecstatic and boisterous right through the long drive home, but a couple of weeks later Lynch got the upper hand again and claimed his fourth consecutive Australian junior title victory at Greenmount from Mark Warren, with Peterson third. The second great rivalry of Peterson's career – the first being with Townend, Bartholomew, McKinnon and any other Coolangatta kids who posed a threat to him – was beginning to take shape, only to be thwarted by Lynch's sudden departure from the competitive scene for several years. There would be many more to come.

Peterson's minor placing in the nationals was enough to get him into the Australian team for the 1970 world championships in Victoria. He seemed to be overawed and overwhelmed and made very little impact at the world titles, but he did make a discovery that was to play a major part in his competitive career: marijuana took the edge off his pre-heat anxiety. As Joe Larkin later told journalist Sean Doherty: 'I was going, Mick, you don't need it, and he was saying, I gotta calm me nerves!'

Peterson soon impressed everyone with his fast, powerful turns and hand jive. He was Nat Young on steroids. as even Young, who had missed seeing him at the world titles, eventually had to admit: 'I remember seeing him surfing Lennox when it had really good banks . . . this kid doing the same sort of thing I was doing, but doing it with even more power . . . Big, strong cutbacks into the pocket, then coming out and doing it again.'

Then surfing in the open division, Peterson took out

> **Peterson soon impressed everyone with his fast, powerful turns and hand jive. He was Nat Young on steroids.**

Queensland's first pro event in February 1971, winning $150 and a quadrophonic stereo player at the Kirra Pro-Am. However, the Peterson era had not quite begun, although the results of the 1971 Australian titles at Bells Beach at Easter certainly indicated that Queensland was fast becoming the new super power with Gold Coaster Paul Neilsen taking out the men's title over his neighbour Peter Drouyn. Peterson bombed out in the quarter finals.

With the world titles scheduled for San Diego in October, the 1972 Australian titles were critical for selection of the team. Although Midget Farrelly and Nat Young had announced their retirement and Wayne Lynch had gone missing, there were literally dozens of surfers emerging as contenders and not all of them were from Queensland. However, two problems presented themselves to the Australian Surfriders Association (ASA).

The first was that several of the better surfers had been called up for national service and therefore could not leave the country without special permission from the Defence department. The second and more immediate problem was that Michael Peterson had been busted for possession of marijuana and a criminal conviction had been recorded. After he convincingly won the Queensland titles at Kirra Peterson should have been first choice for the state team at the nationals, but at a rowdy ASA Queensland meeting he barely survived an attempt to throw him out for being an 'improper ambassador'.

Peterson went to Sydney for the nationals and claimed his first open Australian title, but his drug saga was only just beginning. As Australian champion he led the best national men's team Australia had ever

On his way to winning Bells, 1975. Photo Frank Pithers.

produced for a world championship, with multiple Bells and Australian champion Gail Couper leading the women's squad. The issue for the ASA executive was getting Peterson a US visa, which was not easy with his criminal record. – until someone stumbled onto an interesting fact. Although he had been convicted in a Queensland court under the name Peterson, which was the name of an absent circus worker who had once been the de facto husband of his mother, the name on his birth certificate was 'Philp' and Michael Philp had no problem at all getting a passport and subsequently a US visa.

During 1972 the legend of Michael Peterson grew at pace. Clearly he was the next big thing in Australian surfing and was odds-on with Aussie bookmakers to become the world champion later in the year. The January release of Alby Falzon's landmark surf film *Morning of the Earth* helped drive the legend with a long sequence of Peterson surfing Kirra in the powerhouse style Nat Young had seen at Lennox Head. At some time during the year he ceased to be 'Mick' and became 'MP' to all who knew or revered him. This came about as retaliation from Peter Townend, whom Peterson had christened 'PT'. Both nicknames stuck.

> The issue for the ASA executive was getting Peterson a US visa, which was not easy with his criminal record.

There were some not-so-subtle changes in the MP persona. For one, despite his often strange behaviour he had become a chick magnet, pulling Cronulla femlin Patty Conlon at the Bells event in the first of some notable liaisons with glamorous young women. For two, he had developed a quirky dress sense that combined sartorial elegance with complete inappropriateness. When the Australian team gathered at the airport to fly to San Diego for the world championships, for example, MP wore a suit and tie and polished leather shoes among a sea of floral shirts and jeans. This was around a decade after dressing up to fly had gone out of fashion and possibly was a result of seeing photos of Midget Farrelly and Nat Young in the early 1960s heading off to Hawaii similarly dressed.

The last of that era's amateur world events, San Diego was a drug-fuelled farce. As American journalist John Grissim reported:

> *One hundred and fifty four people booked in [to Travelodge hotel, the event headquarters], 34 more than budgeted . . . In the first 48 hours five hundred dollars worth of towels had been stolen, someone had left two huge garbage bags of seeds and stems in the hallway, twelve hundred dollars in unauthorised room service charges had been written off and a contest volunteer had driven a Ford truck onto the sidewalk outside the lobby, collapsing a large canvas canopy and demolishing a newsstand and three potted palms.*

MP had a wonderful time at the hotel but failed to impress in the surf, while friend and rival Peter Townend made his mark on the world stage by finishing third.

On the way home Peterson and Rabbit Bartholomew stopped in Hawaii for their first taste of big North Shore waves. Peterson surfed well but he never seemed particularly comfortable away, even when most of the Australian team arrived a few days later. Nevertheless, while the rest of the Australians straggled home in small groups Peterson stayed on, living on handouts and occasional cheques from his mother. While he was never able to produce the kind of surfing that made his name in Australia, he became fitter and more aggressive in the water than at any other stage of his career. When he flew home in January 1973 after Joan had wired him the fare he was lean, hungry and ready to pounce. If a timeline is needed for MP's dominance, it began then.

Rip Curl's Doug Warbrick was one of the Australians on the North Shore that winter of 1972–73, following an invitation he'd received from Hawaiian surfing elder George Downing to judge at the Hang Ten American Pro. He recalled: 'At the San Diego world titles I talked to George about a new points-for-manoeuvres system he'd developed for the Hang Ten, and he invited me to come and judge and learn this system.'

Downing's new system was in fact the most radical development in assessing surfing in the sport's relatively short history, removing subjective analysis and replacing it with a template for scoring each element of a surfer's performance. Every wave ridden and every manoeuvre performed added to a rider's score, so the surfer who rode the most and biggest waves and performed the most manoeuvres on them would emerge the winner.

MP with his moon rocket flyer. Photo Stephen Cooney.

Although the system ruled out style and grace as point scorers, many surfers saw it as offering them a clear path to victory, if they were good enough.

Hawaii's Jeff Hakman, then the best competitive surfer in the world, was definitely good enough and he took the rulebook home and studied it for a couple of days, noting in particular the points value of a manoeuvre called the 'zigzag'. This was nothing more than a directional change on the face of the wave. Over the two days of the event at Sunset Beach Hakman zigzagged all over the face of every wave he rode and won easily, proving that you could surf to a plan and win.

When Warbrick returned to Torquay in January he announced a bold plan to take the Bells Beach Classic professional and introduce the points-for-manoeuvres system. His partner Brian Singer agreed, and after some nudging so did the ASA. While theoretically the system offered an equal chance to any surfer with ability who followed the rules, the reality was that it described almost exactly the way MP surfed every time he competed. If there was any doubt that his time had come, this should have removed it.

The 1973 Rip Curl Pro Bells Beach Easter surfing championships, offering $2,500 in prize money and with a whopping $1,000 for the winner, began with an elimination series to select 15 qualifiers from a field of 90 surfers. These would then join 15 invited surfers, including former world champion Midget Farrelly (returning from a brief retirement), former Australian and Bells champions such as Michael Peterson, Paul Neilsen, Ted Spencer and Peter Drouyn, top Hawaiian pro Sam Hawk and Australia's highest finisher at the 1972 world titles, third placer Peter Townend.

Michael Peterson · 57

When the event moved into a final field of 30, the new judging system was explained in detail over a long meeting in the Torquay pub. The first of three rounds began in solid 2 metre Bells waves, with Hawk and Neilsen, who had both surfed in the Hang Ten event and had been at the pub briefing, catching a lot of waves and racking up high points with continual manoeuvres. Peterson, who had also surfed in the Hang Ten but hadn't bothered to attend the briefing, caught four waves and surfed them beautifully but managed to beat only Puerto Rico's Jorge Machuca.

Way down the leader board after the first round, Peterson suddenly focused on the system and how to play it. Rabbit Bartholomew recalled: 'A light globe went on in his head. We were up in the car park and he goes, "If you catch 20 waves and you keep doing turns, you win." It was as simple as that. It took him a while to actually put that into practice, but once he did there was no stopping him.' Peterson stepped on the gas in the second round and pushed into third overall behind Farrelly and Ted Spencer. When Farrelly fell ill and failed to surf the final round, Peterson had no trouble at all in zigzagging his way to victory.

MP after his last big win, Stubbies Pro, 1977. Photo Aitionn.

Peterson won both of the professional events held in Australia that first year of pro surfing, having no problem in cleaning up at home in the Kirra Pro-Am. In 1974, when the Surfabout in Sydney was added to the schedule with the world's largest prize money, he won that as well as Bells and the Kirra Pro then took out the amateur national title for good measure. Over less than two weeks of competitive surfing in the autumn of 1974, Peterson had won more than $4,000 in prize money at a time when the average Australian male yearly earnings were around $7,000. He was on his way to making a living as a pro surfer, even if no one else was.

Having completely mastered the new judging system MP was on a roll, but his behaviour out of the water was becoming so erratic that some of the other surfers were beginning to wonder if there was more to it than simply the influence of marijuana. In fact, Peterson had moved much further along that road than most of his contemporaries knew and was now incorporating LSD and heroin into his regular drug menu, all of which took a bashing as he and Hawaii's Craig 'Owl' Chapman made a manic road trip north from Bells for Surfabout 1974. There was no doubting that Peterson was at the peak of his powers when he won the Rip Curl Pro Bells for the third successive year in 1975, but there was also no doubt that there was something seriously wrong with the legendary MP.

Founded in Hawaii in mid-1976, International Professional Surfing was the first global governing body for professional surfing, and it belatedly put together a championship tour of existing events that resulted in Peter Townend becoming the first world pro champion despite not winning a rated event that year. Peterson

> **The truth of the matter was that the best surfer in the world was an addled, agitated and often angry wreck of a young man.**

won three pro events, two of them unrated, but his win at the New Zealand Pro at Piha pushed him to number seven on the rankings. By his standards it was a tragic result, but many of those close to the action were surprised he even did that well.

The truth of the matter was that the best surfer in the world was an addled, agitated and often angry wreck of a young man., and not even his prodigious drug intake could explain why. Frequently broke despite his healthy winnings, he needed constant financial support from Joan while a new circle of non-surfing friends happily shared the drugs the struggling single mum was paying for. At a time when the southern Gold Coast was a hotbed of drug abuse the mighty MP had become just another guy queuing in the alley for a fix, but he had one last shot in the chamber.

The inaugural season-opening Stubbies pro event in 1977 was the most talked-about surf contest of the early pro era, and those who witnessed it were still talking about it 45 years later. Contest director Peter Drouyn had developed a revolutionary new man-on-man concept to allow the best surfers in the world to go head to head in the best waves in the world, and Burleigh Heads complied by turning on a week of near-perfect surf. The two-man heats provided the packed public gallery with an opportunity to contrast surfing styles and make their own assessments of each wave exchange. Even the inanities of imported announcer, former professional wrestler Lord 'Tally-Ho' Blears, only served to heighten the excitement, and with each elimination round the intensity and quality of the surfing magnified.

Over the final weekend the sun beat down and the surf pumped, and in one of the most exciting finishes yet seen in an Australian surfing event Peterson just managed to beat fellow Aussie Mark Richards. Peterson, who had continued to improve upon astounding performances throughout the event, then gave perhaps his most bizarre performance at a prize giving, disappearing just as he was required then reappearing in a fit of manic eye shifting and arm waving. Artwork preserving the moment still exists on a wall at Burleigh's beachside park.

> **No one then understood …that he was wrestling with the demons of schizophrenia or that this would be the last time he ever stood in the winner's circle.**

MP claimed the $5,000 cheque, but it seemed like the hardest thing he had ever had to do. No one then understood, of course, … that he was wrestling with the demons of schizophrenia or that this would be the last time he ever stood in the winner's circle.

Michael's downward spiral began in earnest in the early 1980s, and it was only when he settled into a life in Joan's care that he seemed to find some inner peace. He eventually made regular appearances at surfing events, reunions and awards presentations, sitting quietly in a corner and acknowledging vaguely familiar faces with his trademark 'G'day, chine.'

Michael Peterson was inducted into the Australian Surfing Hall of Fame in 1992. He passed away peacefully in his mother's arms in 2012.

Classic MP style: floating, about to attack, Stubbies Pro, 1977. Photo Aitionn.

Simon Anderson, Bells Beach Pro, 1981: the first victory on a thruster. Photo Joli.

SIMON ANDERSON

Full name	Simon Anderson
Nickname	Big S
Birthdate	7 July 1954
Place of birth	Manly, New South Wales

Although he never won a world title, Simon helped define surfing's modern era.

In its July 1977 issue *Tracks* magazine featured the line 'Average Anderson' on its cover, promoting its first in-depth profile of surfer and shaper Simon Anderson inside. On one level the magazine had captured the everyday persona of the affable surf star from Sydney's northern beaches just right, but on another level it could not have been more wrong.

By 1977 Anderson had already proven himself to be one of the most stylish and powerful surfers in the world, and by the early 1980s he had also established himself as the surfboard designer who had changed the face and direction of modern surfing with his legendary three-finned 'Thruster'. Anything but average.

Granted, Anderson never won a world title – like Michael Peterson before him he juggled the world tour with surfboard-shaping commitments – but he finished in the top 10 for three years with a best result of third in the world in 1977, the year in which he also won the Australian professional surfing championship. He remained highly competitive into his middle years in the 1990s and 2000s in the World Masters Surfing Championship, but it was as a surfboard design innovator that he made his greatest mark.

Simon Anderson was born in July 1954 at Manly Hospital, the second of three sons for George and Doreen Anderson, who lived not far from the beach in the suburb of Balgowlah. When Simon was aged just five the family had a windfall that changed the lives of the Anderson boys.: George shared first prize in the jackpot lottery, and the £3,000 prize money enabled him to buy a house on the beachfront at Collaroy.

A printer by trade, George made time to swim in the ocean every day and encouraged his boys to do the same. Simon and his older brother Mark soon became natural watermen, body surfing and riding rubber surf mats. There was a slight detour when Mark proved to have exceptional skills as a swimmer and started to train with former Olympic coach Don Talbot. As Anderson told me in 1977: 'Dad made me tag along. We'd get up at five every morning and he'd drive us out to Talbot's pool at Auburn in the western suburbs, where you'd jump into a cold pool and swim your guts out for two hours then drive home to go to school. Mark seemed to enjoy it but I never did.'

While Mark made a serious name for himself in competitive swimming, Simon dropped out and focused his energy on the surf. He recalled: 'I didn't go home and say, "Look, I want to be a surf bum", but that must have gone through their heads. Back then I think most parents thought there was no future in being a surfer.'

When Simon was aged just five the family had a windfall that changed the lives of the Anderson boys.

Anderson already had a board, or at least half a board. He shared ownership of a 9'6" log with Mark, but with his brother at the pool most of the time it was his to drag up the beach to North Narrabeen, where most of the good surfers seemed to congregate. Using a ploy common to parents in the 1960s, when Simon turned 13 his parents gave him his first new surfboard, a blue Fleetfin department store log that was redundant within six months. However, he was ecstatic about it until he learned that it came with the condition that he focus less on surfing and more on improving the below-average mid-year report card he had just received from Narrabeen Boys High. Of course, that was never going to happen.

While Mark was preparing to represent Australia in the 200-metre freestyle at the 1968 Mexico City Olympics, Simon was more frequently absent from class with mysterious ailments that could only be cured by spending long hours in the surf at Narrabeen, where he

'Average Anderson' in his car at Narrabeen, 1981. Photo Aitionn.

would usually find slightly older schoolmates and local surf heroes such as Col Smith, Mark Warren and Grant Oliver. By that time Simon had graduated from the Fleetfin to a shorter Bill Wallace, and from there to the ultra-short boards that were suddenly dominant. Despite his growing size he felt comfortable on the new boards, and after joining the North Narrabeen Boardriders Club and beginning to shine at the junior level he was accepted as a local hot rat.

By Year 10 school was becoming an intolerable distraction from his surfing, and as soon as he had squeaked a pass in the School Certificate Simon left and took a job fixing dings at the Shane Surfboards factory in nearby Brookvale. The gig had been organised by shaper Terry Fitzgerald, who became an early mentor. 'I was stoked,' Simon recalled. 'Thirty bucks a week and I was working in the surf industry!'

His parents didn't share the enthusiasm, but that year of 1971 turned out to be his breakthrough in competitive surfing and they began to come around. Simon took out the Sydney junior title and followed it with a third in the New South Wales juniors. Eligible to compete in the nationals at Bells Beach but still not quite one of the boys, Simon caught two trains to Geelong and a taxi to Torquay, near the contest site, where Geoff McCoy's team took pity on him and let him sleep on the floor of their rented digs.

In good waves at Bells Simon amazed himself by taking out the Australian junior title against much more fancied opposition. Typically, he still couldn't quite believe it when he was interviewed six years later: 'It was a total mystery to me. Andrew McKinnon was the best junior by a mile, and Peter Townend had more polish than I did, but they had bad luck and I got the win.'

The following year he won both the state and national junior titles from rising young star Mark Richards and was an automatic selection for the world titles in San Diego, the farcical event that would be the last hurrah for the amateur world event for many years. With surfers behaving badly all over the Travelodge event headquarters, the big teenager bombed out early

Simon receives his first Surfabout winner's trophy and cheque, 1977. Photo courtesy Shane Stedman.

in the surf and spent much of the contest locked in his room with Narrabeen teammates watching the novelty of colour TV and drinking beer. Even a week in Hawaii on the way home couldn't convince him that world travel was much more than just a hindrance, a view that later coloured his approach to the world pro tour.

Although he made the podium in neither state nor national titles in 1973, when pro surfing made its Australian debut at the Rip Curl Pro Bells Beach Simon drove down for the event with the Narrabeen crew. He finished third in the open division behind Michael Peterson and collected $250 for the effort. It was his first cash win, but he was already convinced there wasn't enough money in the sport to go round. The it boy of 1972 went back into contest limbo and didn't fully emerge for four years. Anderson put this down to becoming happily locked into the Narrabeen scene, 'drinking too much, living from week to week without much ambition'.

Even a late-season trip back to Hawaii in December 1974 didn't break him loose from the Narrabeen code, and he returned 10 days later contemptuous of the North Shore scene. On the other hand, his

> **The it boy of 1972 went back into contest limbo and didn't fully emerge for four years.**

reputation as an emerging surfboard shaper was building momentum. He knew he was getting better board by board, and being a test pilot for his own designs made him think more about the hydrodynamics of man on board. On his third trip to Hawaii in 1976 Anderson got himself back onto the international radar with some impressive free surfing at Sunset Beach that earned him an invitation into the Smirnoff Pro. Unfortunately, poor wave choice saw him exit the event early, but it gave him a taste for the new International Professional Surfers (IPS) World Tour.

After five years with Shane Surfboards Simon had gone into business for himself along with partner Garth Cooper in Energy Surfboards, and he knew he'd have to devote a lot of time to building the business. He also understood that he needed to build the brand, and the best way to do that was to juggle his tasks and make time to compete in as many as possible of the eight rated events scheduled for 1977.

Simon Anderson · 67

Simon off the lip at North Narrabeen. Photo Aitionn.

The year didn't begin well. The inaugural Stubbies pro was the most hyped event in pro surfing's short history, and every star in the firmament was there to win it. Anderson had been off the beer for five weeks and felt fit and relaxed on his fine-lined Energy single fin. In good waves at Burleigh Heads he cruised through the first round against new junior star Cheyne Horan, but in the second South Africa's Shaun Tomson – about to become his biggest rival that year – had his measure. Out of the event with a $200 cheque, Anderson pointed his battered Holden south, told Narrabeen sidekick Dave West to navigate and drove straight through to Phillip Island in Victoria for the next event, the Alan Oke Memorial. Another early exit. It was going to be make or break at the Rip Curl Pro at Bells.

His recent poor results meant that Simon had to win entry to the main event through the Quiksilver Trials, and fortunately a new board he'd shaped for Bells arrived by freight the day before. Thinner and wider and with harder rails than he was used to, the board was magic under his feet and he won the trials with ease, then he went on to win the main event. With a $4,000 cheque in his wallet he headed back to Sydney for the Coke Surfabout, the last and richest event of the Australian leg of the world tour. With one win apiece in rated events Michael Peterson and Simon were leading the IPS rankings, but Simon found he still had to surf his way through the non-seeded elimination round. When he saw that Midget Farrelly, coming back from a long retirement, was seeded ahead of him his determination to win became even more steely.

Although the Surfabout was anti-climactic, held almost from start to finish in barely contestable knee-high waves, it was ironic that the biggest surfer in the event surfed the best, extracting enough power to unleash huge turns and even find a barrel or two. The only surfer to trouble Simon's road to victory was the smallest surfer in the event, young Cheyne Horan, but no one was going to stop the ascent of Average Anderson. As reported in *Tracks*:

> *Simon Anderson is dressed, as he always is for social occasions, in his wall-blending uniform of brown and white check sports shirt, fawn jeans and desert boots.*
>
> *The occasion is the presentation of awards for the 2SM/Coca Cola Bottlers Surfabout, the richest surfing contest in the world, in which Simon has taken out first prize of six thousand dollars. As his name is called he ambles to the microphone and accepts his cheque with an aw-shucks toss of the head. A speech is called for because not only has Simon won the Surfabout, but he has been named the Australian Professional Surfing Champion for 1977.*
>
> *He has a crackly voice and when he's nervous it misses notes. He quickly thanks sponsors and officials and moves to the meat of his message. 'I'd like to thank the Narrabeen locals for their support and encouragement', he says, tilting his head in the direction of a table littered with debris and empty beer jugs, around which the ordinary blokes of Narrabeen are seated. As Simon leaves the stage, they lead the cheering. They are especially proud tonight because one of their own is receiving the accolades.*

After winning back-to-back Australian tour events in 1977, laid-back Simon Anderson was suddenly recognised as being one of the world's leading surfers at the top of the rankings in front of Shaun Tomson and Rabbit Bartholomew. He had won $10,000 in the space of a month, and his dad George got on the phone to former Australian cricket captain Bob Simpson to seek advice about how to manage Simon's growing profile. After so much scepticism from his parents and himself it now seemed they were all on the same page: there was a future in pro surfing. Simon paid back the $3,000 his brother Mark had loaned him to start Energy

After winning back-to-back Australian tour events in 1977, laid-back Simon Anderson was suddenly recognised as being one of the world's leading surfers.

and invested the rest in airline tickets for the rest of the IPS tour. He knew it was a gamble, but he couldn't turn his back on the very real possibility of becoming the second IPS world champion and of

Simon, North Narrabeen, 1990. Photo Joli.

A trademark layback. Photo Aitionn.

promoting his surfboard brand into the stratosphere.

So the reluctant jetsetter was off to South Africa, where Anderson finished a respectable fourth in the Gunston 500 in Durban. Shaun Tomson won the event, which put him into the ratings lead. Things got worse the following week when Anderson was bundled out in the first round in tiny conditions at Umhlanga Rocks, further widening Tomson's lead. A few weeks later in Brazil Anderson was taken out in the first round again, this time by Peter Drouyn, and his world title hopes were over despite a late-year revival in Hawaii to make the final of the Billabong Pipeline Masters.

Finishing the IPS tour that year in third position was hardly a bad result. In fact, it was the best rankings result of Anderson's career, but financially it was crippling. Third in the world was still good for selling surfboards, but he realised he couldn't continue to follow what had become his world title dream while being financially responsible for a business back home and for his world travel. Simon had no cash sponsor, as most of the surfers on tour had. The solution came in the sale of Energy Surfboards to shaper Steve Zoeller, who rehired Simon as a shaper and designer. This enabled him to continue touring while earning a living during his breaks at home.

A further problem was that as the tour evolved more of its stops outside Hawaii were at predominantly small wave breaks,

On the beach at Bells, 1977. Photo Joli.

for which Simon was not ideally physically suited. In response to this, other surfer/shapers on the tour began to develop their own equipment changes. Having been inspired by Hawaiian veteran Reno Abellira's surfing on a twin-finned fish shape in tiny waves during the Surfabout in Sydney in 1976, fellow pro Mark Richards had started shaping and riding twin fins in competition and was suddenly unbeatable on them.

However, Simon just didn't feel right on them, as he revealed in his autobiography *Thrust*: 'I'd been on tour since 1977, getting my arse kicked in small waves. Twin fins had been around for a while and MR had been dominating on them, but they never really worked for me. The tour was going to all these small wave locations and I'd reluctantly ride a twin fin . . . out of necessity . . . Jumping from one board to the other was really doing my head in . . . It was a real problem.'

Anderson plugged on, finishing 19th in 1978 and 15th in 1979 then improving to sixth the following year. One day in October 1980, home on a break from the tour, he spotted Sydney shaper Frank Williams emerging from the surf at Narrabeen with a twin-fin board

'Jumping from one board to the other was really doing my head in . . . It was a real problem.'

that had an additional small keel fin centred on the back. It wasn't the first tri-fin board he had seen, but it got him thinking about the extra stability that could be achieved. He went back to his shaping bay at Energy and started making himself a new board. What eventually became known as the Thruster incorporated Frank Williams's basic idea – although Simon's extra fin ended up being the same size – and Geoff McCoy's no-nose, front-end design. The particular unique combination of elements created a new benchmark in performance surfboards, one that still dominated surfboard design more than 40 years later.

The Simon Anderson Thruster did not make its creator a fortune, nor was it immediately widely accepted as the design of the future. After being largely ignored at an American trade show booth devoted to the new design, Simon's US collaborator Gary MacNabb told him: 'You're going to have to win a contest on it.'

Simon took this advice to heart when the 1981 Australian tour began, but he was knocked out in the first round of the Stubbies in small, dribbly conditions at Burleigh Heads. On the long drive south for the Rip Curl Pro he prayed for surf and had his prayers answered: and then some! Bells produced perfect huge waves for the early rounds, and Anderson unleashed a power attack the likes of which had never been seen. at the break. Finding an extra few metres of forward thrust out of his bottom turns, he snapped off the top of the massive waves and set up for a repeat performance, eventually winning the event from Cheyne Horan. The Thruster had arrived, and when Anderson backed up by winning the Coke Surfabout in much smaller surf the following week there was no question about its application in all conditions.

Simon finished sixth in the world in 1981 and continued to surf in tour events over the next few years without matching that level of success again. He quietly retired in the mid-1980s. At the same time, however, his shaping career flourished and he married Sharon, and together they created a loving family. He never took out a patent

Bells produced perfect huge waves for the early rounds, and Anderson unleashed a power attack the likes of which had never been seen.

on his Thruster design and didn't believe it was his right, claiming all along that it had come from multiple influences that included Frank Williams and Steve Zoeller. In much later years various friends and fans tried to ignite a fund to send 'a dollar for every Thruster you've ever owned' to Simon Anderson, but the man himself just shrugged and never bought into that, feeling more than satisfied with the career he had enjoyed as a pro surfer and one of the world's most respected surfboard designers.

Simon continued to surf competitively at local and club level well into middle age, then reinvented himself in the late 1990s in world masters' championships in Mexico, Fiji, France, Ireland and Hawaii, where he competed with distinction and great spirit. Approaching the age of 70, he still enjoys surf safaris up and down the coast, and his trademark dry wit has only grown drier and funnier with age.

Still got it at 64! Competing in the World Masters in the Azores, 2018. Photo courtesy Azores Tourism.

Mark Richards in perfect symmetry at Off the Wall, Oahu, 1977. Photo Dan Merkel.

MARK RICHARDS

Full name	Mark Richards
Nickname	MR, Wounded Seagull
Birthdate	7 March 1957
Place of birth	Newcastle, New South Wales

The ultimate competitor, Mark Richards won four world titles by also being surfing's ultimate stylist.

Although he seemed destined for greatness from a very early age, Mark Richards may never have achieved his Australian record of four consecutive world professional titles had it not been for watching a technically brilliant display of competitive surfing from Hawaiian pro Reno Abellira at North Narrabeen on Sydney's Northern Beaches during the Coke Surfabout contest of 1976.

In its third year, the Surfabout offered the richest prize purse on the fledgling world tour. Midway through the event 19-year-old Richards took the lead in the multi-round contest, but it was held over a very long period and inevitably the swell died. Running out of time, the organisers elected to proceed in tiny waves. Abellira, one of the most savvy competitors on tour, pulled out his secret weapon: a 5'7" wide-tailed twin fin.

I was on the beach that afternoon when the small-framed Abellira mesmerised a big crowd with a flawless display of manoeuvre-packed rides that the tall and lanky Richards could not hope to match. He watched from the competitors' tent as the small, wide twin fin hugged the shape of the better sections and floated through the flat spots, allowing the Hawaiian to stack up the points. Richards managed to hold on to a reduced lead and ultimately win the event – his first major professional victory – but the lesson of Reno's twin fin stayed with Richards and was filed in the overflowing surfing intelligence part of his brain.

Mark Richards was born in the industrial seaport of Newcastle, New South Wales in 1957, the first and only child of Ray and Val Richards. Ray had a successful car sales business on Hunter Street in the centre of the city's commercial district, but he'd been a beach person all his life and every spare moment he'd spend with his young family on one of the city's attractive beaches. Although he'd ridden various paddleboards in his time as a lifesaver before a debilitating hip injury caught up with him, Ray had never tried the modern Malibu board that had recently been introduced to Australia. However, before Mark was six years old he'd been given a scaled-down version – a

> The lesson of Reno's twin fin . . . was filed in the overflowing surfing intelligence part of his brain.

MR classic off the top turn on a Brewer Lightning Bolt, 1976. Photo dickhoole.com.au.

At Off the Wall, North Shore, Oahu, 1978. Photo Jeff Divine.

6 footer with GT stripes – and his dad was pushing him into waves.

Mark's skill sets improved rapidly when the family took their annual vacation at Coolangatta, where the little boy would spend all day riding the long, gentle waves of Greenmount. He was a natural, and as soon as Ray realised his son had talent he began to take a greater interest in what had become known as the 'surf craze' to the extent that he started to buy boards from Sydney manufacturers and feature them on the walls of his vast car showroom. Soon surfboard sales were so great that he had to get rid of the cars.

One of Richards's fondest memories of a happy childhood is accompanying his father on surfboard-buying trips to the manufacturing centre of Brookvale. While Ray negotiated his price with pioneer board builders such as Barry Bennett, Bill Wallace and Scott Dillon, Mark wandered around to the factory side and marvelled at the sight, sound and smell of surfboards being created. Although he didn't share it with his family, he was formulating an idea about his future.

At the age of 12 Richards joined the Merewether Surfboard Club and got his first taste of competition. I shared waves with him at Newcastle

Mark Richards · 79

Intensity seen from the water, Off the Wall, 1978. Photo Jeff Divine.

Point on several occasions that year and was in awe about the dexterity of the kid, whose backside turns were already razor sharp. He was difficult to engage: he was painfully shy, and if you said 'Hello' he looked as though he might burst into tears. The rough and tumble of competition soon knocked that out of him.

In 1970 Richards began his assault on the record books. Still a cadet at 13, he competed against older boys as a junior and finished second in the New South Wales schoolboys and third in the junior division of the state titles. The following year he finished second in the state juniors and in 1972 he took out the state title and finished second in the national juniors, which won him a slot in the Australian team for that year's world amateur championships in San Diego.

Richards travelled to the event chaperoned by surfboard shaper Geoff McCoy and Newcastle surfer Roger Clements, and while he didn't make a mark on the leader board at the notoriously ramshackle event he became acquainted with the surfboard designs being generated by the likes of Barry Kanaiaupuni, Dick Brewer, Reno Abellira and Ben Aipa both there and during a short stopover in Hawaii on the way home. While McCoy was an unabashed BK fan,

Richards just loved the fine-line pintails of Brewer and the new sting models of Aipa. In 1971 he started riding the stubby twin-fin fish boards that were sweeping Australia but tired of their performance limitations, and after meeting the Hawaiians he switched to variations on Aipa's single-fin sting.

By that time Richards was well and truly on the international radar, prompting Ray Richards to soften his stance on his son's schooling. As Mark told *Surfer* magazine in 1980: 'I used to sit there and think, what has this A, B and C got to do with life?' However, he respected his parents enough to actually attend 'unless the surf was really, really good', and he was actually a good if reluctant student. In 1973, while Mark continued at school, Ray became his unofficial manager and the family travelled together to big events around the country. In one successful year Richards won both the state and national junior titles.

So confident was Ray Richards in his son's ability that he allowed him to leave school to pursue his dream. As it turned out, 1974 was a tough year with a victory in the local Mattara contest the only bright spot, but at its end Richards rode the

> 'I used to sit there and think, what has this A, B and C got to do with life?'

giant waves of Hawaii's North Shore for the first time.

Although he didn't place in the two events that winter, he impressed the elder statesmen of the sport with his courage and humility. This would stand him in good stead over the next couple of seasons as the other young Australian pros became embroiled in bitter and sometimes physical conflict with some of the Hawaiians. Richards was held up as a shining example of sportsmanship and left to concentrate on winning events, which he did in some of the biggest waves ever contested. During the 1975 Hawaiian season he won the Smirnoff Pro at big Waimea Bay and the World Cup at Sunset Beach, taking home $9,000 in prize money: a huge amount at the time. The gangly kid had arrived on the international stage.

The year 1976 was when a world championship pro surfing tour became a reality, but at the start of it the surfers didn't know they were competing for ratings points. The new Hawaii-based International Professional Surfers (IPS) hurriedly and retrospectively announced the tour events mid-year, prompting many of the would-be pros to buy round-world airline tickets they could ill afford to play catch-up at the remaining events.

Richards was having none of it. He'd already worked out a plan to combine a shaping career – he was given his first electric planer at the age of 13 and had been developing his skills ever since – with professional surfing and his love of the homebody lifestyle. He competed in the Australian events during autumn and the Hawaiian events at the end of the year, giving himself a full six months of the year at home to build his shaping business. Ironically, his placings in those events were enough to give him a decent income, and his travel expenses were much lower than those of the other pros. It might make it harder for him to win a world title, but he could handle that – for now.

In 1978 Richards described his lifestyle in an interview with *Surfer*:

> *I live in Newcastle . . . [S]mack bang in the middle of the city is a giant steelworks, which produces most of Australia's steel, plus we export a lot of coal to Japan. The air isn't too healthy, but it's a fun place to live; plenty of people, plenty of average waves and plenty of places to go at night. It's great, I like it. I live on the street that runs down the middle of the main business area, on top of our surf shop. Out of my bedroom window I have a panoramic view of the ships in the harbour and the smokestacks; out the kitchen window is one lonely tree, so I can tell the wind direction. Home's home, no matter what! Oh, and I don't go anywhere without my portable stereo. I have one beside my bed, one in my car, and one in my shaping room.*

Fast becoming a surfing idol for his goofy personality as much as his incredible surfing skills, Richards endeared himself to young readers in that interview. When asked what made him happy, he quickly responded: 'Sex and tube-rides,' which became a surfer catchcry around the surfing world. In a profile article titled 'Mr Humble Finishes First' in *Surfer* in 1980 the emerging side of his personality was revealed: 'Once he was painfully shy, but his self-assurance has grown in leaps and bounds. He greets everyone with the same bouncy hi and a manic grin.

Another perfectly executed lip bash, North Shore, 1976. Photo Dan Merkel.

When he talks he looks the object of his attention directly in the eyes. Once a funny, gangly kid, in maturity he has become a thoroughly pleasant fellow, a straight shooter.'

Richards had been dubbed the 'Wounded Seagull' for his unique wide-armed style as he glided across all parts of the wave in a smooth, flowing movement, but what was little known beyond the pro ranks was that Mr Humble could also engage in the heavy stuff when he had to. In 1979 he told *Surfer*:

There are people who use guerrilla tactics and people who go past that. In the final of the Pipeline Masters Larry Blair paddled directly in front of me on one wave, and tried to paddle me off on an angle. I grabbed his leg and squeezed it. I thought if I can't catch this, you won't either. [Larry] Bertlemann did that to me too. As I paddled I punched his leg, over and over. Nothing was being said, just a heavy vibe.

Richards finished 1976 at number three on the new IPS rankings behind fellow Australians Peter Townend and Ian Cairns, which validated his stance on competing part time, although he was more interested in what he was learning about shaping than he was in rankings. In a torrid year for Aussies on the North Shore, Richards was considered to be the most respectful and respected of the foreign pros. Over a two-month stint honing his shaping and design skills alongside Dick Brewer, he developed a network of friends and contacts among the Hawaiians that surpassed anyone else's.

Following the Surfabout event in Sydney in May 1976, Richards had been so impressed with his surfing on a twin fin that he sought advice from Reno Abellira as to what measurements would work for him. As he told an interviewer: 'I made a five-ten swallowtail winger with fluted wings and a full, round nose. This board worked well in surf up to four foot, and that winter in Hawaii I spoke to Dick Brewer about twin fins. We decided to make one a little longer and narrower than the one I'd been riding, another swallowtail winger that was proportionately more like a regular board.'

Richards said later of master shaper Brewer: 'He taught me the A–Z technique of how to shape a board. Up until then, I lacked the method. The ideas were in my head, but my hands couldn't produce. Brewer taught my hands to catch up to my mind.' The twin-fin journey had begun. As Richards said:

Modelling for Quiksilver, 1978.

The Immortals of Australian Surfing · 84

I rode that board in the 1977 Surfabout. It was my small-wave slop board for the remainder of that year, but I was still surfing an Aipa sting in bigger waves. Later that year I flashed that if my six-two twin worked so well in small waves, maybe longer and narrower versions would work in bigger waves. I took a six-four version to Hawaii that year, and for the first two weeks of October, I surfed it nonstop at Chun's and other smaller waves, then used it for my first session at Sunset. Amazingly it worked so well I tried to build a seven-four twin to surf at Sunset when it got bigger. It was a disaster, so back to the drawing board, but I knew the idea had great potential.

Richards finished second to Michael Peterson at the inaugural Stubbies Pro at Burleigh Heads in a memorable final in 1977, but the IPS tour had grown and competing only part time meant Richards slipped back to fifth place in the rankings. The following year he didn't even make top five, but in 1979 he came out with new intent and a quiver of twin fins plus a few rounded single fins for really big days.

Following a victory at the season-opening Stubbies Pro and his second consecutive Bells title, Richards realised he would have to chase the title at fresh battlegrounds and won the first event of a new Japanese tour. He was in the box seat for his first world title, but while he went home to Newcastle defending champion Rabbit Bartholomew and fellow Australian Cheyne Horan followed the tour. After events in Japan, South Africa and Florida they had both edged ahead of Richards.

At the start of the Hawaiian season Richards was back in fourth place, with just two rated events left for him to reclaim the lead. While playing down his passion for the prize, he approached the contests with serious intent. Unfortunately the season began problematically, with the organisers scheduling both the rated Billabong Pipeline Masters and the unrated Duke Invitational on the same day to take advantage of a good swell. Richards and other competitors found themselves racing along the beach to make their heats at Pipe and Sunset Beach with moments to spare, but Richards won the Duke and finished fourth in the Masters to keep his title hopes alive.

He sealed the deal with a fourth victory for the year in the World Cup over 1976 world champion Peter Townend, whose wily tactics almost threw a spanner in the works. The part-time pro was the world champ, having surfed in only nine of 13 events on the tour. The plan had worked with slight modifications, and Richards took it into his title defence in 1980. Having fought so hard for his first, Richards cruised to his second title, winning four events in Australia, South Africa and Hawaii. The 1981 and 1982 seasons were somewhat closer but ended with the same result.

Having broken all the records with his four consecutive world titles, the genial 'MR' called time on the tour. – he had nursed an increasingly painful back injury through the last season – and a sizeable group of contenders breathed a huge sigh of relief.

According to pro-surfer contemporary Michael Tomson, Richards's dominance of the sport on the twin fin over his title years was so great that several surfers, Tomson included, simply gave up and left the pro tour. Although other surfers took multiple titles through the 1980s, no one approached the unstoppable competitive machine powered by two

Having broken all the records with his four consecutive world titles, the genial 'MR' called time on the tour.

fins that was MR until the emergence of Kelly Slater in the early 1990s.

For all the fear he inspired in his rivals, the softly spoken Richards was humble, shy and almost timid on land and he rarely made enemies. Even fellow Australian Cheyne Horan, who finished a close second to Richards in three title races, said he found it difficult to muster any ill will towards the champion even though he alone had stood in the younger surfer's way. Typically, Richards confessed years after retiring from the world tour that he felt genuinely sorry for thwarting Horan's championship aspirations.

There were further chapters to come in the MR story. He married his schoolteacher girlfriend Jenny in Newcastle and started a family while building his surfboard business with sales around the world and the continued sponsorship support of major surfwear companies. The sponsorship along with his truly competitive nature are probably what made him continue

The Immortals of Australian Surfing · 86

Inside a perfect Burleigh barrel, 1977. Photo Aitionn.

to compete selectively, mostly in Hawaii, through the 1980s, showing he had lost none of his edge. He won back-to-back Billabong Pro Championships on Hawaii's North Shore in 1985 and 1986, defeating new-generation champions Tom Curren and Gary Elkerton in big, challenging surf. As noted by surf historian Matt Warshaw, this was 'a competitive surfing career epilogue that has no equal'.

And he wasn't done yet. In 1993, 10 years after Richards had quit the world tour, he was asked in a *Surfer's Journal* interview with Warshaw if he missed it. He said: 'I really, really miss it. Every time I pick up a magazine and read about where the guys are, I really want to be there. I miss being a player, and I don't know if I'll ever get used to it completely.'

> As noted by surf historian Matt Warshaw, this was 'a competitive surfing career epilogue that has no equal'.

Mark Richards OAM receives another award. Photo Joli.

Helping out at Surf Groms. Photo Surfing Australia.

A few years later that opportunity arose with the development of a World Masters Surfing Championship for former pro surfers. Richards warmed up with a second placing in France and then won another world title in Ireland in 2001 at the age of 44. I have unforgettable memories of the middle-aged MR unleashing his trademark swoops off the lip and power turns under it in the messy, windswept waves of Bundoran in County Donegal. Still beautiful to watch.

After the conclusion of the Quiksilver Masters series in Hawaii in 2003 Richards stayed on with what was then the world's biggest surfwear company, headlining its Silver Edition promotional team of surfing legends. However, the constant travel, mostly in Europe, was wearing on the homebody with the crook back and he always looked forward to getting home to Newcastle.

In 1989 Jenny and Mark lost a child to sudden infant death syndrome, and for many years the couple and their three children used the MR star power to raise funds and create awareness about the tragic condition. Now well into his 60s but still surfing and shaping, Mark Richards continues to help local Newcastle charities, and as one of the two first inductees into the Australian Surfing Hall of Fame he remains one of surfing's finest ambassadors.

The little master at his peak, poised at Pipe. Photo Jeff Hornbaker.

TOM CARROLL

Full name	Thomas Victor Carroll
Nickname	TC
Birthdate	26 November 1961
Place of birth	Sydney, New South Wales

Throughout a storied career punctuated by incredible highs and painful lows, 'TC' has remained Australia's favourite pocket rocket.

When a freckle-faced micro grommet from Newport Beach on Sydney's Northern Beaches peninsula won the inaugural Golden Breed Pepsi Pro Junior during the January school holidays of 1977, *Tracks* magazine got so excited about it that it turned its February edition into the 'kids' issue'.

The reason for the excitement was the stellar performance of Tom Carroll, a 15-year-old goofy footer about to start Year 10 at a local high school, in powerful North Narrabeen waves that were well overhead – for him. Squeaky of voice and not yet grown to the towering 1.7 metres he would reach, as noted by *Tracks*

'Tom amazed spectators with his nutcracker cutbacks and heavy inside cover-ups.' The magazine later nominated him the 'hottest emerging talent of the year'.

Although this was the first time Carroll had rated serious media exposure he had been amazing contest watchers for quite a while, winning the New South Wales state schoolboys at the start of 1976 and following up with a third place in the junior division at the state titles. Asked by *Tracks* if he would be pursuing a professional surfing career following his pro junior win and $500 prize money, he laughed and said, 'I'd love to. Maybe not straight away though. I think I should be a bit older.'

Just the following month he made his professional debut in the open ranks at the inaugural Stubbies Pro at Burleigh Heads, courtesy of a wildcard entry for his pro junior win. In a star-studded field he was eliminated in a close contest by rising Hawaiian star Buzzy Kerbox. It didn't matter: Tiny Tom had started to make his mark.

Carroll was born in November 1961 in Sydney, the son of a leading newspaper editor, and was raised in the beachside suburb of Newport. He began surfing at the age of eight, a few months after his mother died of pancreatic cancer. The youngest Carroll child, after brother Nick and big sister Josephine, Tom never lacked for love and support at home and particularly from Jo, four years his senior, when Vic Carroll was working long hours for the Fairfax newspaper group. He and Nick also sought solace in the waves they found in front of their Newport Beach house.

For Christmas 1969 Vic gave Tom a little compressed foam coolite board, while Nick got a rubber Surfoplane. It didn't really matter, as neither of them could stand up on their craft. Then one magic day before the summer was over Tom got to his feet. 'I stood up, just like

Breakthrough moment: Tommy about to surf the final of the 1977 Pro Junior. Photo Martin Tullemans.

that!' he told his biographer Kirk Willcox. 'And then I went down. It was an amazing feeling.' Nick ditched the Surfoplane for a coolite with a rubber fin, and the Carroll brothers were away.

Nick was the first to get a fibreglass board, a dog of a thing that Tom borrowed and snapped. Vic took the brothers to the nearest surfboard factory, Ron Wade Surfboards at Mona Vale, and soon Tom was on his own Wade. Although Vic Carroll was a senior publishing executive making good money he wanted his boys to understand the value of a dollar, so they both had to work before and after school to help pay for surfboards and bikes – which more or less worked until surfing completely took over.

The older Newport surfers, including future pro Derek Hynd, wouldn't allow the groms to surf the Peak, the best wave on the beach, so they along with the Carrolls responded by joining the surf club and competing in their Malibu board events. Soon they were claiming their rights to the Peak, and Tom began to attract attention further up the peninsula when he was invited to join the Peninsula Boardriders at Palm Beach. In 1975, when Derek Hynd started a club called Newport Plus, Tom and Nick joined and it was soon the hottest contingent of juniors on Sydney's north side.

Neither brother seemed particularly naturally gifted, but they were both enthusiasts from an early age. Tom was determined to kick every wave he caught into submission. At first there was a lot of energy and not much style, but by the

Tom was determined to kick every wave he caught into submission.

time he had become the star surfer of Newport Plus and was making an impact at state junior level, Carroll was developing into an explosive goofy who could smoothly link his moves in the manner of one of his mentors and soon to be his surfboard sponsor, Narrabeen's Col Smith.

At the end of 1977 Vic Carroll relented and allowed his younger son to leave school, having completed the School Certificate. At the age of 16 Tom went off to labour on a building site, hoping to secure a carpentry apprenticeship; he lasted three days. He did better as an apprentice panel beater, working four days a week at Narrabeen and attending technical college one day a week for more than a year.

In early 1978 Joe Engel, a new mate Carroll had befriended at the first pro junior, came down from Queensland to compete in the second and stayed with the Carroll family at Newport. This may have been a tactical mistake because the chunky little natural footer beat Carroll in the final, establishing a friendly rivalry that lasted through their careers. In May, having downed tools in the panel shop, Carroll repaid the favour, beating Engel in the final of the Australian juniors division in big surf at Margaret River in Western Australia.

Carroll also competed at the Stubbies Pro and the Rip Curl Pro at Bells Beach that year without success, and stayed in the panel shop when others were chasing tour glory overseas. He remembered being particularly annoyed when Cheyne Horan, another young Sydney rival, won his first pro event in Brazil, telling Vic, 'I could have been over there winning that.'

The $500 cheque Tom had received for his only pro win so far had gone into the bank towards his first trip to Hawaii, the venue for all surfers' dreams. back then plus some of their nightmares. Although he had some misgivings about riding monster waves the experience of winning at large Margaret River had given him a degree of confidence, although a knee injury incurred in big surf on the New South Wales central coast that year had kept him out of the water for six weeks. In October 1978 he landed in Honolulu ready for business, picking up a new quiver of Simon Anderson shapes from the oversized baggage counter.

The $500 cheque Tom had received for his only pro win so far had gone into the bank towards his first trip to Hawaii, the venue for all surfers' dreams.

Although he didn't enjoy competitive success that North Shore season – he was eliminated in the first round at the pro class trials – his long learning curve in waves of consequence had begun. I found the young surfer just after dawn one morning gazing out to sea from Rocky Point and taking photos with a borrowed camera as he made his decision where to surf. At the end of the season I was nominating him in a short list of people with whom the 'future of surfing will lie' in an article for *Surfer* magazine called 'The Changing of the Guard'. That may have been premature, but it was correct.

Carroll became a full-time professional surfer in 1979, the year brother Nick confirmed his own surfing credentials by winning the New South Wales and Australian titles. Tom lost the final of the pro junior to Joe Engel again, and failed to make the same impact that contemporaries such as Cheyne

Second Pro Junior win, 1980. Source unknown.

Horan and Chris Byrne were having in the open events. He did, however, manage fifth place in the Chiba Pro on his first Japan trip.

Soon after his return from Japan, Carroll suffered a horrendous stomach injury when a friend's board speared him with the force of a bullet while surfing Newport Peak. After emergency surgery to repair the multiple tears, he spent two months out of the water recovering in the first of a long series of injuries that would threaten his career. Come November, he was back in Hawaii for his second season. Competing in the Pipeline Masters for the first time, he made the final but finished last.

In his rookie year on the International Professional Surfers' (IPS) world tour rankings he came 24th and made total prize money of US$750. It wasn't looking too promising, but at least he had the panel beating to fall back on!

At the other end of the IPS rankings was Australia's Mark Richards, winning the first of his four consecutive world titles while transforming the parameters of performance on a twin-fin surfboard. Like the majority of the touring pros, on occasions Tom was also soon riding a twin but the other aspirants to a world title would have to wait in line until MR had finished with them.

Slowing things down a tad at Chopes. Photo Joli.

In 1980 Carroll claimed his second pro junior title and finally started gaining some traction on the main pro tour, particularly after some stronger results in Hawaii. He improved his ranking but didn't quite make the seeded top 16. The following year he finished fifth at the Stubbies and third at Bells, but missed the Hawaiian leg of the tour to recover from knee surgery. After a remarkable comeback early in 1982, it was in Japan where the changing of the guard finally came to fruition at the Marui Pro, described by surfing historian Matt Warshaw as the 'bellwether event of the year':

> The surf, for once, was good – overhead and offshore . . . the top story at the contest was the man-on-man finals pairing – the first exchange between 20-year-old Australian Tom Carroll and Tom Curren, an 18-year-old from Santa Barbara. The two surfers were easy to tell apart. Carroll, the goofy-footer, was short and freckled, with speed-skater thighs, a barking voice, and a brightly-airbrushed board. Curren was the slender regular-footer on the white board who rarely said a thing. The Aussie was favoured, but not by much. Curren [the current world amateur champion] was the hottest rookie to come along in years; this was just his second world tour event, and here he was in the final. Carroll rode the best two waves but didn't have a good third score. Curren was smooth and steady from beginning to end, and the five-man judging panel split three-to-two in his favour.
>
> Everybody at Chiba that day understood the significance. Curren and Carroll were by no means the only hugely gifted surfers on the world tour, but they clearly represented the sport's future. Everything you needed to know about surfing's performance trajectory for the decade could be graphed on Tom Carroll's muscle-flexing turn combinations and Tom Curren's ethereal flow and technique.

After a string of good results, including a second at Bells to Richards, Carroll claimed his first major victory at the season-ending World Cup in Hawaii. He finished third in the IPS rankings behind Mark Richards and Cheyne Horan and the stage was set for greater things, but there were a few clouds on the horizon. While no one doubted Tom's potential for greatness, his competitive performances were erratic and he was not then regarded as a tactician. Some of this was put down to the fact that he had become a renowned party boy whose increasing cocaine use did not indicate he was taking his career completely seriously, and right after his second at Bells he was called into the Torquay offices of major sponsor Quiksilver and sacked. It was a devastating blow personally and financially, but it did have the effect of getting him focused on surfing – at least temporarily.

Another reason for Carroll's new focus was that he had hired his first personal manager, Peter Mansted, whose military style put off sponsors but seemed to work on Tom, and a new sponsor in surfer Shaun Tomson's Instinct brand. Thus armed, Carroll went after a world title.

In 1983 the IPS tour was superseded by the Association of Surfing Professionals (ASP), which gave the surfers themselves some ownership of the tour although the downside was that the surfers had to get accustomed to a new mid-year start and finish. Carroll surfed well throughout, but was still behind Rabbit Bartholomew in the rankings going into the final three Australian events in early 1984. He won all three, bringing his year's event wins to six and thus becoming the first ASP world champion. His title defence year proved much tougher, but at year's end he scraped over the line in front of Shaun Tomson with just two wins from 24 events.

Quiksilver's million dollar man.

The snap heard around the world: Pipeline, 1991. Photo Joli.

In 1985 the two-time world champion was on a roll. Fame and money had arrived simultaneously and with it constant media attention, powerful cars driven too fast, endless parties and, of course, drugs. While the full extent of Carroll's drug use was not revealed for a couple of decades it was an open secret in surfing's cognoscenti, and it may have contributed to the suddenness of his shock announcement to a journalist a couple of days after the annual Bells binge: 'I've decided not to compete in South Africa this year,' he said. 'I feel it's important for me as world champion to take a stand on apartheid.'

While the journalist scribbled madly, brother Nick and manager

Total backhand control at Sunset. Photo Jeff Divine.

'I've decided not to compete in South Africa this year. I feel it's important for me as world champion to take a stand on apartheid.'

Mansted, both completely blindsided, stared into space. 'We haven't worked out the details,' Mansted finally bluffed with masterful understatement. 'We were going to announce it at a press conference next week.' Of course, by this time there was widespread support for sporting boycotts of South Africa's apartheid regime, but not in surfing – and not at the Instinct office, where brand founder Shaun Tomson, Carroll's major sponsor and South Africa's own surfing legend, was apoplectic.

History proved Carroll right and even in 1985 he was not alone in his stand, being joined in the boycott by surfers Martin Potter and Tom Curren. At a time when Carroll alternated between strict training regimes and long cocaine-fuelled party programs, coming out on an important issue such as apartheid was something of a cleansing of the soul for a young man who could seem shallow and self-obsessed at times but had a much deeper side. It also won him a friend in new Australian prime minister Bob Hawke, who noted some years later that he could find 'no example in the history of Australian sport where a champion has been prepared to put principles so manifestly in front of his or her own interests'. However, nothing could salvage his Instinct sponsorship. Fortunately, Mansted was already working on a new plan.

Carroll finished third in the world in 1985, second in 1986 and fourth in 1987. No longer world champion but still a contender, his reputation as a surfer of incredible ability in all kinds of surf but particularly in waves of consequence only grew, and in 1988 his manager negotiated a groundbreaking five-year, million-dollar exclusive contract with Quiksilver. The prodigal son had come home with surfing's richest sponsorship agreement in his pocket.

Surfing's first million-dollar man earned his keep, remaining in the top five in all but one of his remaining years on tour. despite suffering several debilitating injuries, of which a surfboard up the anus was easily the most embarrassing and almost the most dangerous, winning back-to-back

Pipeline Masters titles and claiming the Hawaiian Triple Crown of Surfing. Carroll had 26 career pro tour event victories over a 14-year career, including Pipeline Masters wins in 1987, 1990 and 1991, but contest victories were not seen as his major value to sponsor Quiksilver, by then the world's biggest and richest surf company. Carroll became a global brand ambassador and full-time surf adventurer, seeking out mid-ocean reef breaks to conquer or presiding over a boatload of high-maintenance groms while a branded video was made.

Prime Minister Hawke, along with world champions Kelly Slater, Wayne Bartholomew, Mark Richards and Nick Carroll, took to the podium at Tom Carroll's world tour retirement black-tie dinner. Hawke said: 'There is no Australian sporting hero or legend at whose name I have a greater surge of affection and admiration than [that of] Tom Carroll. Thank you for what you've done for your sport. Thank you for what you've done for your country.'

As historian Matt Warshaw noted: 'Some speakers got a laugh while making reference to Carroll's career-long assortment of injuries, including a surfboard-inflicted stomach rupture, a concussion, two knee

Surfing's first million-dollar man earned his keep, remaining in the top five in all but one of his remaining years on tour.

injuries requiring major surgery, and, most famously, a perforated rectum suffered after being speared by the nose of his board.'

Possibly the hardest blow of Carroll's life came on the afternoon before the finals of the 1987 Pipeline Masters, when he learned his older sister Josephine had been killed in a car accident. The close-knit Carroll family was devastated by the loss of the much-loved Sydney celebrity chef, and Tom phoned his father to say he would come home immediately. 'No,' Vic said, 'stay there and win. It's what Jo would have wanted.' And that's what Tom did.

In the 2000s Carroll and long-time Quiksilver teammate and friend Ross Clarke-Jones became tow-surfing partners, and over the ensuing years they charged some of the biggest, scariest, mid-ocean waves ever ridden, turning their death-defying feats into a film and television series. This might have been the bravest thing Carroll ever

Taking time out to consider the future: Narrabeen car park, 1977. Photo Aitionn.

did in a daredevil life but in 2013 he surpassed it with the publication of *TC*, a book co-written with Nick that tells the full story of Carroll's career-long battle with drug addiction, including a tragic period of crystal meth abuse that cost him his marriage. He wrote:

> *I did all sorts of things to try to score, because it was pretty scarce. It brought me into contact with some really seedy people. People who died doing it. A guy I knew committed suicide. That was a really frightening thing because I realized that was where it leads, that was the end point. But understanding what happened to that person didn't stop me. It wasn't me, after all. It didn't happen to me. The nature of the beast is to keep going until it stops.*

Clean and sober since 2007 and a regular attendee at Narcotics Anonymous meetings wherever he finds himself, Tom Carroll and partner Mary live not far from where he grew up, meditate, eat healthy foods and stay very fit. He remains close to his three grown daughters and, now in his 60s, still surfs like a man possessed.

Mick Fanning slices into J-Bay, South Africa, 2002. Photo Joli.

8

MICK FANNING

Full name	Michael Eugene Fanning
Nickname	Eugene, White Lightning
Birthdate	13 June 1981
Place of birth	Penrith, New South Wales

Mick Fanning has overcome every obstacle in his path to become the quintessential 20th-century Aussie surf warrior.

It's a peculiar irony that a surfer of such incredible natural ability and tactical cunning as three-time world champion Mick Fanning will always be best remembered for the worst day of his life. 'I will never forget the day,' he told a media outlet a few years later:

It was Sunday, 19 July 2015, and I had woken up feeling great. I was in South Africa competing in the J-Bay Open, the sixth event on the World Surf League [WSL] Championship Tour. I was in the final against a really close mate, Julian Wilson. The winner of the event would take the ratings lead in the world title race, and I really felt like I was on my way to victory that day.

Around four minutes into the final, things got . . . interesting. A great white shark appeared. Things happened so fast. I punched and kicked out at the shark, trying to get away. I thought I was going to die. I guess everyone watching on from the beach that day, and on the live broadcast all over the world, thought the exact same thing.

I was one of those viewers, watching from Australia very late on a Sunday night, and I will never forget that long, drawn-out moment either. The night had started out so promisingly, settling back with a cup of tea to watch the all-Australian final in perfect down-the-line conditions. While Jeffreys Bay can often look grey and imposing, on this glorious afternoon of blue skies and clear green water it looked positively benign – and then all hell broke loose.

Julian Wilson had taken the first wave to open his account, while defending J-Bay champion Fanning waited for a set further up the line. As Wilson paddled back out the cameras focused on Fanning, who was paddling as a wave approached. Fanning suddenly seemed confused about which direction to paddle in. 'You can see a little splash,' commentator Joey Turpel said in a strange monotone.

'Holy shit!' fellow commentator and former world champion Martin Potter cursed over the top of him. A glimpse of fins, Fanning thrashing, then lost from sight as a wave obstructed the cameras. These were some of the longest seconds imaginable, particularly if you knew either or both of the competitors. Then it was over. As Wilson paddled hard towards the shark to help his friend and rival, the shocked but unharmed Fanning managed to scramble to safety on a patrol boat.

A glimpse of fins, Fanning thrashing, then lost from sight as a wave obstructed the cameras.

The event was called off, with both surfers sharing second place points and prize money. For surfing it was an historic and horrific first. For Mick Fanning, overjoyed to be alive, it was a life- and career-defining moment.

In the immediate aftermath Fanning appeared relaxed and cracked wise with the boat rescue crew before telling the WSL video cameras: 'I was just sitting there. I was just about to start moving, and then I felt something grab, got stuck in my leg rope. I instantly just jumped away, and then it just kept coming at my board. I was kicking and screaming. I just saw fins. I didn't see the teeth. I was waiting for the teeth to come at me as I was swimming. I punched it in the back.'

Fanning explained that he was pulled under by his leg rope, and when that broke he 'started swimming and screaming. I can't believe it. I'm just tripping . . . To walk away from that, I'm just so stoked.' Of course, he was in deep shock, which he soon began to

Fanning plays to the crowd at the Quiksilver Pro, Hossegor, France, 2010. Photo Joli.

realise: 'I was on the water-safety boat chatting with everyone and laughing about the whole situation. At that point it was so surreal. But once I got on land and saw the reaction from everyone who had witnessed what went down, it hit me. The hugs I felt from some of my close friends brought out a different feeling. I realised then just how lucky I was.'

That year of 2015 turned out to be Mick Fanning's ongoing nightmare, from which close friends despaired he would survive. It would take the mettle of a true champion to make it, but Mick had one great advantage: he'd been a battler since the beginning.

Born Michael Eugene Fanning to an Irish father and Australian mother in the outer western Sydney suburb of Penrith in 1981, the youngest child with three older brothers and a sister, Fanning's first home was in Campbelltown, even further away from the coast. He grew up on various parts of the New South Wales north coast, including a short stint in Coffs Harbour living with his father John after his parents' marriage broke up when he was aged just three. Thereafter the family of five kids of single mother

Mick Fanning · 107

and psychiatric nurse Liz followed her career to Ballina and finally to Tweed Heads, just south of the Queensland border. Wherever they lived Mick tagged along to the beach with his older brothers Sean and Ed and had his first surf at age five, but it wasn't until the family settled at Tweed Heads when he was 12 that he started to ride a board in earnest.

As Mick noted a few years ago: 'My three big brothers had started surfing and, as little annoying siblings tend to do, I followed them. My competitive nature really started to take hold when I hit double digits – soccer, running, school, cricket, rugby league – the game didn't matter, I loved it all; but surfing was different. I got a buzz from surfing

A new Coolie Kid showing his style in 1999. Photo Joli.

I couldn't get from anything else.' Interviewed about his mother's influence by a women's magazine, Mick opened up for the first time about Liz:

> My mum is a kind-hearted person. She was strict with us five kids, but fair. She put our needs above her own, which was selfless . . . Dad always cared for my siblings and me, and was present in our lives, but Liz raised us as a single mum, which wasn't easy. She figured if she had a house close to the beach, her four sons would go surfing and stay out of trouble. Mum drove an old Land Rover. My brothers and I would pile in the back with our boards and she would drive us to junior tournaments, go about her day, then pick us up. She'd watch if she could. To her, it didn't matter if we won or lost. She just wanted us to be happy and have fun.

As a surfer Mick was a fast learner, scoring a third in the national juniors four years later then winning the Pro Junior at the age of 18 in 1999. Alongside his best mate at school and in surfing Joel Parkinson and Dean Morrison, the trio became known as the new 'Coolie Kids', a homage to the 1970s pioneer pros and Coolangatta residents Michael Peterson, Peter Townend and Rabbit Bartholomew. Like them, the Coolie Kids were fast tracked to the top through club contests at the Snapper Rocks Surfriders Club, but it was Parkinson and Morrison – particularly the smooth-as-silk Parko – who made a bigger impression in those early years, both winning a major pro event ahead of Mick. Parkinson won the Billabong Pro at Jeffreys Bay in 1999 to become the youngest winner of a world tour event at the age of 18, while Morrison was Queensland and Australian amateur champion in 1998 and won the Pro Junior in 2000.

Everyone who watched him surf the long line-up at Snapper Rocks that was becoming known as the 'Superbank' knew that the white-haired, athletic Mick was poised for success. However, first he had to get over a huge emotional hurdle. In 1998 older brother Sean, who was Mick's inspiration and a talented, aspiring pro surfer himself, was killed in an horrific car accident along with another popular Coolangatta surfer. The deaths rocked the Gold Coast surfing community and completely devastated Mick. When he could function again, he told friends he was now absolutely committed to making it as a pro 'for Sean'. Years later he told *Men's Health* magazine:

> *Sean and I had the same goals and it bound us; we dreamed of making the world tour together. He encouraged me and looked out for me. He was my hero. He was just 20 when he died. We were out at a party together but got split up. I walked home . . . Sean jumped in a car with friends. On the walk home the police picked me up and told me Sean was gone. I was burdened with the news and had to tell the family. I locked myself in my room and didn't leave it for a week. When I finally got myself together my motivation to achieve my goals went into hyperdrive. I wanted to honour my brother by fulfilling our dream.*

That was his mission when he was offered a wildcard into the Rip Curl Pro Bells Beach in 2001 by his new sponsor Rip Curl. Fanning was in devastating form though still only aged 19, revealing a flowing, fast and powerful attack to win the event from Byron Bay's Danny Wills. Accepting the unique bell trophy for his first world tour event victory, he dedicated it to Sean then went on to win that year's World Qualifying Series and earn a place on the World Championship Tour for 2002. Fanning won his first Billabong Pro Jeffreys Bay in 2002, finishing the year fifth in the world and being named rookie of the year by the Association of Surfing Professionals (ASP).

Patience is a virtue for any surfer, whether it's having the self-control to wait inside the last minute of an important heat for the bomb that is going to win it for you or it's the perseverance required to almost reach the top of your profession and hang there interminably while waiting for the opportunity to go that final step. In Fanning's rookie year his best mate Joel Parkinson finished second in the world on the ASP rankings and seemed destined for a world title, perhaps ahead of Mick, but Hawaii's Andy Irons took his first title in 2002 and signalled the beginning of almost a decade of the greatest rivalry between two champions that the sport had ever seen – and neither of them were Australian.

With a record six world titles to his credit in the 1990s, Kelly Slater had retired from touring in 1999. In the new century he was back

Right on the foamball at Cloudbreak, Fiji, 2013. Photo Joli.

with renewed energy and just one ambition – to beat Andy Irons. Irons won three consecutive ASP world titles before Slater hit back, winning the next two years. In the meantime, Mick Fanning had to hang in and wait, battling bad luck and serious injury.

Fanning's surfing was fast, exciting and at times even electrifying, earning him the nickname 'White Lightning'. He had a competitor's intelligence that enabled him to focus at the right times and put together winning heats and in Australia at least, the dogs were barking that he would soon be a world champion, but then fate intervened.

On a surfing boat trip in the North Sumatran islands in 2004, the champion in waiting floated a section on a head-high wave just as he'd done a million times but, as he told his biographer Tim Baker: 'As I came down I tail-dropped, my back foot came off and I did the splits. Then the wave landed

A study of style, concentration and timing, 2013. Photo Joli.

on me and pushed me further into the splits and almost through my board. My hamstring muscle ripped clean off my pelvic bone.' Fanning was in agony through two days of travel home, where the news was not good: he was out of the water for six months and faced a long journey back to fitness.

Rehabilitation was long and painful, but remarkably Fanning came back fully fit at the beginning of 2005 and took out the season opener, the Quiksilver Pro Gold Coast, at his home break of Snapper Rocks, then went on to win the Rip Curl Search Pro on Reunion Island to finish the year in third place and poised for a title. The only thorn in his side was Kelly Slater, almost 10 years his senior but in devastating form and racking up more and more victories. Fanning took out two more events in 2006, including his second title at J-Bay, but could not keep pace with Slater and finished third again.

Then came the real test of a champion: could he shrug off disappointment and refocus? Over the ups and downs of his early career Fanning had developed a reputation as a wild party boy, albeit one who could switch gears swiftly from binge drinking to serious event training. This split personality was alluded to in the title of his second video release, *Mick, Myself and Eugene*, but there were plenty of stories about Eugene's behaviour doing the rounds.

As surf historian Matt Warshaw noted: 'He'd become notorious for beer-fuelled antics at banquets and parties. At the 2005 Surfer Poll Awards [in California] he wandered onstage to heckle Kelly Slater during his acceptance speech. To win his first world title, Fanning cut back on his drinking, hired a trainer, put a new level of torque into his frontside off the top, and discovered a monomaniacal level of focus.'

In 2007 Fanning won the Quiksilver Pro Gold Coast again, then the Quiksilver Pro France. He was ratings leader going into the Billabong Pro Mundaka, and as

> 'He'd become notorious for beer-fuelled antics at banquets and parties.'

Mick feeling right at home at Kirra. Photo Joli.

Mick Fanning · 113

I watched that event from the old stone steps above the picturesque break I realised I had never seen a more focused surfer before his heats, blocking out the world with his big headphones, pacing like a caged tiger and willing himself to win. He didn't, but when he took the next event in Brazil the crown was his. In eight of 10 contests that year Fanning made the semis or better, winning three events. As he told *Men's Health*:

> *On the day I won my first world title in Brazil there was a dolphin out there in the line-up. It wasn't part of a pod, it was just cruising around solo and kept popping up during my heats. I felt the presence of my brother, Sean. That day I became the first Australian to win the title since Mark Occhilupo eight years earlier, and the greatest of all time, Kelly Slater, handed me the title trophy. It was the best, and I got to dedicate it all to my brother.*

If Fanning took his foot off the accelerator a little in 2008 it was perhaps understandable. In 2004 he had met model Karissa Dalton, and after several years of sharing a house they tied the knot in 2008. Seemingly settled and happy, Mick came out

Enjoying the good life, Tavarua, Fiji, 2014. Photo Joli.

guns blazing at the start of the 2009 season with another world title in his sights but he hadn't taken into account the long-thwarted world title ambitions of best friend and rival Joel Parkinson, who dominated the first half of the season by winning at Kirra for the Quiksilver Pro and at Bells Beach and J-Bay.

Undaunted, Fanning fired back in the second half with consecutive victories at Trestles in California, at the Quiksilver Pro France and at the

The Immortals of Australian Surfing · 114

Rip Curl Search Pro in Portugal to take his second title, but it came at a price. As Fanning said later: 'I locked horns with my best mate in an intense title race. I won the title but it took its toll on me. Joel and I didn't exactly hang too thick that year. I was winning but felt like my relationship and friendships were suffering.'

Fanning's 2013 title was a model of consistency, as Matt Warshaw observed:

> *He finished in the top five of nine of the year's 10 events, including a win at the Quiksilver Pro France. Heading into the final event of the year, the Pipe Masters, eleven-time world champ Kelly Slater was the only surfer with a chance of catching Fanning. Needing a semi-final berth to claim the title, Fanning squeaked past Yadin Nicol in the dying seconds of their quarterfinal clash, clinching his third world championship, and becoming the fifth male surfer to win at least three titles.*

This was not the first or the last time a surfer won a world title through consistent high placings rather than wins, but Warshaw was one of several commentators who took the gloss off Fanning's achievement:

> *Slater won the Masters in devastating form, and because he took out three events total for the year, to Fanning's one, many observers felt that he was in fact the year's standout performer . . . Plan the year so that you have at least a small margin of error at the end. Sound a bit clinical? Exactly. That's Fanning all over. He marched through the season, event to event, with the grim certainty of a man who knows full well that Pipe is not where you want to make a world title stand.*

Fanning saw it in a different light, later telling an interviewer:

> *The third world title was more fun. I could flick the switch and get into competitive mode but could now zone out and enjoy the world around me. Competition became a game and it started a solid run for me. I was in contention again for a few years and 2015 felt like another world title year.*
>
> *At J-Bay I felt unbeatable, and going into the second half of the year I eyed this as my event to charge ahead on the ratings. That's when old mate in the grey suit popped up and in a matter*

of seconds altered the course of my life and gave me perspective I'd never had before. Competition points didn't mean much in that moment. Living was a priority.

The brush with death at J-Bay was actually the second of a trio of tragic events that befell Mick Fanning in 2015. The first was that his seven-year marriage to Karissa was falling apart; the couple divorced in 2016. The third was that at the end of the year older brother Peter, 43, died of an enlarged heart. It was the second brother Mick had lost after Sean in 1998. After J-Bay Mick took a break from the tour, but he returned in time to be a contender for another world title. He recalled:

I went into the final event, the Pipe Masters, leading the world title race. Everything felt right . . . a fourth title was right there. On the day it was all set to go down at Pipe I was woken early, too early, by a knock on my door. My beautiful mum standing there . . . tears in her eyes and clearly hurting. She told me Pete had passed away.

That morning friends were comforting me and telling me I didn't have to go out if I wasn't up to it. I knew what Pete would want. To win the world title I had to place ahead of Brazil's Adriano de Souza. I was up for the challenge but had to overcome the two greatest Pipe surfers of all time in Kelly Slater and John John Florence. The waves were firing and we all had excellent rides. I won the heat but lost the title to Adriano. Losing the title didn't hurt. At the end of the day I only had Pete in my thoughts.

Fanning later told an interviewer: 'That was the one that just floored me. I was like, what else can be taken in a year?' At the end of 2015 he hit rock bottom, explaining: 'I felt like I had nothing to give myself, or to the people around me, or to family or friends. I just didn't see a way of coming back. I've never felt that empty before. I just lay in bed, did nothing, wouldn't leave the house.'

Fanning took time out and travelled the world with the Rip Curl Search team on a wave hunt that also became a soul-searching mission. By the start of the 2016 season he still didn't feel ready to compete but knew he had a date with destiny at Jeffreys Bay. The return to the scene of the previous year's near tragedy

Fanning's frightening experience in South Africa and his subsequent return was front-page news.

was profitable: he beat Hawaii's John John Florence in the final and got the shark off his back. Still undecided about his future as a competitor, Mick was back in 2017 but the fire was gone. He said: 'I saw glimpses of the future performances of Florence and Filipe Toledo. I saw the kind of hunger and determination it takes to get yourself into title contention with Gabriel Medina. I don't have that drive for competition anymore.'

At the Rip Curl Pro at Bells Beach in 2018 Fanning announced his immediate retirement, and in 2017 he went public about his relationship with speech therapist Breeana Randall. In 2020 the couple had their first child, son Xander, and announced their engagement.

After the shark attack at Jeffreys Bay, Fanning became a student of shark behaviour and later helped make the documentary *Save This Shark* with shark conservationist Cristina Zenato. He has remained active in the anti-culling movement and other conservation causes.

As successful in business as he was in the waves, Fanning has built up a sizeable property portfolio and in 2016 co-founded the Gold Coast–based Balter craft brewing company with Joel Parkinson and other surfing partners, three years later selling it to Carlton and United Breweries for around $200 million. In early 2022 Fanning and Parkinson took time out from surfing and business to activate their jet skis in the Northern Rivers area in New South Wales to rescue people from their homes in record-level flooding.

Mick Fanning · 117

Pam's trademark grace and power bottom turn, 1990. Photo Aitionn.

9

PAM BURRIDGE

Full name	Pamela Burridge
Nickname	Pammie
Birthdate	26 July 1965
Place of birth	Sydney, New South Wales

Poised, self-assured and naturally talented on a surfboard, this was no airhead surfie chick.

In 1999, after she'd retired from the women's world professional surfing tour for the second and final time, Pam Burridge was described by *Surfer* magazine in the US as 'the Mother Superior of women's surfing'.

Did they mean Mother Teresa? Pam had certainly mentored and nurtured other competitors over her long time at or near the top. Or were they being ironic, because whatever she may have been over the highs and lows of her roller-coaster 15-season career — tomboy, puffy-cheeked punk rocker, failed pop singer, alcoholic, anorexic, glamour queen and country gal — the 1990 world champion had never been a head nun.

Sweetheart Pam Burridge caused a sensation when she burst onto the women's pro scene in 1980 aged just 15, but she soon showed she was no airhead surf chick. In fact, the Manly teenager was poised, self-assured, articulate and naturally talented on a surfboard. A promoter's dream, she was jumped on by the Australian media, which had been starved of an Aussie surf queen since Mooloolaba 'shark sheila' Kim McKenzie — a good part-time pro who attracted international attention in the early 1970s for her other job as a shark catcher — had retreated to her fishing boat.

Reflecting on how much surfing had changed over the years in the 200th issue of *Tracks* magazine in 1987, writer and former national champion Nick Carroll observed: 'The '80s, so far anyway, has definitely been a decade in which women have pushed their surfing boundaries further than ever.' The women may have been surfing better but by the end of the decade – Burridge's first on tour, when she battled not only her opponents but her own demons and the continued male dominance of her sport to reach the top. – you could still measure the advances their sport had made with a wooden ruler.

Since the birth of Australian pro surfing at Bells Beach in 1973, when the men competed for $2,500 and the women for a trophy and a Golden Breed windbreaker, women had been the poor cousins in pro surfing around the world despite the emergence of a string of promotable champions such as Hawaii's Margo Oberg and Lynn Boyer, California's Kim Mearig and Floridian Frieda Zamba.

Australia's pioneer female surfing champion Gail Couper recalled: 'When Bells went pro it made no difference to the women. We didn't see any of the money! Maybe a special award or two, but it really didn't make a difference. Rip Curl didn't sponsor girls for years. I don't think there was any worthwhile money for girls until Pam Burridge's era, or even later.'

In her first decade on tour, Pam battled not only her opponents but her own demons and the continued male dominance of her sport to reach the top.

It was certainly still tough for women when Burridge went pro. The International Professional Surfing (IPS) world tour, in just its fifth season, had in its first year only crowned a men's champion. In 1980 only the Rip Curl Pro at Bells Beach and the World Cup in Hawaii included a women's division, and there were no stand-alone women's events. The prize money was pathetic: US$10,000 of an aggregate of US$239,000.

It was only when surfers such as Hawaii's Laura Blears and South Africa's four-time world pro champion Wendy Botha posed nude for *Playboy* that the male-dominated sport and its male-dominated media took any notice of them. Even when *Surfer* magazine ran a cover story titled 'Ladies of the Sea' over more than 20 pages in 1980, they profiled many of the top women but ran much bigger photos of swimsuit

Butter wouldn't melt in her mouth: Pam, aged 14, at Avalon Beach. Photo Bill McCausland.

models who had nothing to do with surfing. This was the world 15-year-old Pam Burridge entered in 1980, but it was all she ever wanted and she was talented and tough enough to survive and ultimately thrive.

Burridge was born in July 1965 to computer programmer Bill and housewife Irene Burridge, the third of three daughters spaced about seven years apart. The Burridges, who lived at Clontarf on Sydney Harbour just above Manly, were a sporting family. Bill's antidote to long hours behind a primitive, room-sized computer screen was running, and he became a highly competitive marathoner. By the time Pam was a toddler her mum Irene was spending a lot of time poolside with big sister Donella, who was developing into a champion synchronised swimmer destined to represent Australia at the 1984 Los Angeles Olympics.

Pam's early sporting pursuits were also framed around the racing lanes of a pool, where she showed considerable promise, but already she was exhibiting a fiercely independent spirit that led her to the beach. Despite being a natural in the water, she hated the whole idea of water ballet and despised team sports. As she told *Tracks* magazine a few years later: 'That was one of the appeals of surfing for me, that individual nature of it. At school I could only play netball and I hated netball. So when surfing came along I dropped everything else.'

As writer D.C. Green observed in a 1998 profile:

> She was upset when she learned that, because she was a girl, she would never be allowed to play for the Manly Sea Eagles. Seeking an alternative adrenaline release, Pam graduated from her skateboard to a KFC coolite, which she would ride across the backyard pool, to a bulky five-foot-eight single-fin shaped by a family friend – a present Pam eventually succeeded in badgering from her parents for her 10th birthday.

The following summer Pam enrolled in the Warringah Shire Council's surf school at Freshwater that was run by photographer and surfing jack of all trades Bill McCausland. She was the only girl in the class, although few of the boys realised that. As she told *Wahine* magazine years later: 'I was uncomfortable being a girl. Nobody who I surfed with knew I was a girl for about two years. I kept my mouth shut, so I didn't get hassled. I didn't have any older brothers to protect me.' No, but she had McCausland, who saw her promise from the start and became her first surfing mentor.

Having graduated to her first custom surfboard, a Barry Bennett, at the age of 12 Burridge started competing with Manly Pacific Boardriders, which actually had a girls' division. Of course, she won it as the youngest competitor, attracting the first media attention of her surfing career in *The Manly Daily*. Still just 12, she got another burst of publicity after competing against the boys at the 1978 Golden Breed Pepsi Pro Junior at North Narrabeen. The pro junior had made its debut with only a boys' division (which was won by Tom Carroll) and was an instant success, attracting the best grommets from all around Australia. Pressured to include girls in 1978, the event struggled to get the numbers to fill two barely noticed heats, in which Pam came out on top. She also surfed in the boys' division, and although she finished second last in her heat it had been noted that here was a girl who could really surf.

Representing the Australian Women's Surfing Association with pioneer Isabel Letham, 1978. Source unknown.

Also in 1978, in a brave move Queenslander Gail Austen led a women's breakaway group called the Australian Women Surfriders' Association (AWSA), the goal of which was equal rights in surfing. Austen, a successful businesswoman, got high-profile pioneers Isabel Letham (who was taught to surf by Duke Kahanamoku at Manly in 1914) and 1964 world amateur champion Phyllis O'Donell to become patrons of the new association, attracting considerable media attention.

The first AWSA contest was held in August 1979 at Newport Beach, with Burridge winning by a single point from Wollongong's Sharon Holland, who'd finished seventh in the professional ranks the year before. The AWSA event made all the Sydney papers, with the women's lib storyline getting more column inches than the actual surfing, but their point was being made loud and clear.

Even before that, 1979 was shaping to be the year everything clicked for Pam. In February she won the Moovin' On junior series and backed that up by winning the New South Wales open women's title at the tender age of 14. She was signed up for the prestigious McCoy surf team, joining her idol Cheyne Horan, and Geoff McCoy himself shaped her a board – only the third custom board she'd owned.

Suddenly she was a media darling; even hard-bitten *Tracks* paid attention. While she didn't enjoy it much she could see that the publicity was working. In the summer of 1979 she signed on to do a lucrative campaign for surf

Pam focused on completing the move, Coke Classic, Narrabeen, 1991. Photo Joli.

> **When he sang his hit 'Two Tickets to Paradise' [Eddie] Money danced to the front of the stage, crouched down and locked eyes with Pam for the duration.**

brand Crystal Cylinders, which was huge at the time. 'It happened so quickly,' she told an interviewer. 'And it just seemed to never stop from that point. I was pretty stoked, but I think my ego got a little wild there for a time.'

Pam got her first taste of rock stardom that summer when a radio station arranged for touring star Eddie Money to take a surf lesson at Freshwater with coach Bill McCausland, for whom Pam was working as an assistant coach. Money was more interested in Pam than he was in learning to surf, and the teenager found herself being invited along with McCausland and his wife to catch his concert from the front row. When he sang his hit 'Two Tickets to Paradise' Money danced to the front of the stage, crouched down and locked eyes with Pam for the duration.

In 1980 the AWSA held their first stand-alone Australian titles on Pam's home beach at Queenscliff. The then ubiquitous goofy footer beat a field of more than 50 women from around the country to win her first Australian title. Surf journalist Sean Doherty wrote: 'The contest was as much a statement as it was a surfing contest. The matriarchs of Australian surfing presided. Phyllis O'Donell judged, while Pam was handed the trophy by an elderly lady in a tweed coat and bowls hat. "That was the first time I'd met Isobel Latham," recalls Pam. In the years ahead, Pam and Isobel would become close, with Pam naming her own daughter Isobel.'

Pam's 1980 Australian title doesn't appear in the record books because it wasn't recognised by the Australian Surfriders Association, the official Australian titles of which were held that year in South Australia with just a handful of women competing. While her unofficial title also didn't get her to the world titles in France it did win her an invitation to compete in a couple of pro-am events in Hawaii, travelling with her mum and fellow surfer Pru Howarth. To compete Pam had to pay $50 to join the IPS, which made her Australia's first official female pro surfer and gained her a ranking of number 11 for the year. It also made her persona non grata in the amateur ranks but, undeterred, she said farewell to her schoolmates as she quit Mackellar Girls High and joined the pro tour in 1981. She finished her rookie year in fifth place within the group of just 16 women professionals.

Australia had yet to claim a women's world professional championship, but it seemed like just a matter of time. As D.C. Green said:

> *[In 1982] Pam bolted from the blocks, held on through the season, and with one event to go was leading the title race. Though she placed ahead of nearest rival Debbie Beacham at Haleiwa, the results for the world title were reversed by one of those quirky mathematical technicalities that would become a hallmark of Pam's career. Debbie won, Pam finished #2. 'I was heartbroken, but at least I still had something to strive for,' she reasoned.*

There was plenty of striving over the years to come, not to mention frustration and heartbreak as the surfing public and media turned on Burridge for not giving them what they wanted – nay, demanded. Over the next four years she finished third three times and second again in 1986 at the age of 21. This last was particularly hard to take since she had led the tour going into the last event, where she bombed out in the first round. Her hero Cheyne Horan had suffered the same sequence of devastating near misses under the twin-fin assault of Mark Richards. The monkeys on Pam's back were Kim Mearig and Frieda Zamba who, together or separately, held her from a championship.

Pam Burridge was no quitter, but her seeming inability to clinch the title began to affect her deeply. As she told *Wahine* many years later:

> *Things were changing really fast. It was all twin-fins and it was the beginning of the surfwear boom – the greed of the '80s – that kind of growth without any real soul or direction. But we just went with it and showed up where they told us to show up. I remember the turnover on the women's tour was quite high – you'd get a girl that would have a go, and she might only stay for one year, then fly home, get married, get a job, or go back to*

At the 1980 Rip Curl Pro, Bells Beach. Photo Joli.

particularly after the gloss of 'next world champion' had begun to wear a bit thin. D.C. Green said: 'Pam always struggled for enough [money] to even remain on tour. In the mid-'80s, she went on the dole, worked in a video store, took on unlikely sponsors such as car-parts dealer Asian Wrecks, and even released a tongue-in-cheek single with then-boyfriend Damien Lovelock of the [Sydney punk band] Celibate Rifles.'

The single and video 'Summertime All 'Round the World' by Pam and the Pashions was featured on the children's TV show *Simon Townsend's Wonder World* and created some interest, but it didn't sell and she (thankfully) never got to perform it live. Pam's passion for Lovelock didn't last long either, but the punk phase was around a while. As she told *Wahine*:

> school. I didn't blame them at all. There was almost no money. The only people who were lucky enough to stay around were either at the top or had enough backing to keep on doing it.

Burridge had the ability to remain near the top but that didn't necessarily translate into big sponsorships,

> *After I'd been pro for two years, I went kinda punk. Surfing by that point had already become a job, and I hated being boxed in. The pressure in my life was coming from surfing, and because of that it didn't fill me up like it used to. I loved riding waves, but there was so much about surfing I didn't love. Plus I didn't have that many*

Pam Burridge · 127

friends who were surfers. So I was living two lives. My surfing life, and my nightlife, where I'd go to clubs and see bands and hang out with my friends.

Burridge sought solace from her surfing frustrations in the party life, to which she was well suited, having grown from tomboy to punk to occasional glamour queen and with a bold personality to match her looks. No one had a bad word to say about Pam, but she was not happy with herself and drank too much and partied too

Grown up and with a new approach to competitive surfing, 1988. Photo Aitionn.

hard. According to her biographer Marion Stell she was suicidally depressed for at least six months during 1985, and she was anorexic after several years of carrying a little more weight than peak fitness dictated. As Pam told *Wahine*:

> *There came a point where I'd rather be in a bar than go to the hassle of surfing. I was really run down and started getting sick a lot; my immune system was shutting down. I had a friend [in Hawaii] who had been in a similar position and had a pretty good recovery. She had to cope with exactly what I'd had to cope with. For me it helped to listen to someone who was like me, with the same sort of past, telling me how it happened for her and how she got well. That was a turning point in my life.*

In 1987, when Pam plunged to seventh, her worst ranking since joining the world tour full time, she started dating Mark Rabbidge, a battle-hardened surfer and shaper who had fought his own demons with the bottle. With Rabbidge being 15 years her senior it seemed an unlikely pairing, but he and Pam became soulmates. He inducted her

> 'There came a point where I'd rather be in a bar than go to the hassle of surfing.'

into Alcoholics Anonymous's Twelve Steps program and she started to regain her strength, vitality and surfing spirit. Within a year she was clean and sober and back on track to win the world title.

After finishing second in 1988 and 1989 she began to feel the need to reset her entire approach. Part of that was in response to a new rivalry with South African Wendy Botha, who had won the first of an eventual four world titles in 1987 – Pam's dog year – and was on her way to a second in 1989 and had relocated to Australia and resettled at Avalon Beach, just north of Pam's home base. An aggressive, in-your-face competitor, Botha was now in Pam's face wherever she surfed. Burridge badly wanted to beat Botha, but she knew she had to internalise her feelings.

Pam told *Wahine*: 'I had to work on a new approach to my contest surfing. I finally figured out that I didn't handle pressure well at all. In fact, I probably have the absolute opposite personality type to what

I need to be a competitive sports person – I'm way too introspective, and if I get close to a goal, I think, "Well, I'm gonna lose it now."'

In surfing, an element of self-belief is having faith in your equipment, but remarkably Burridge remained riding McCoy single fins into the mid-1980s – long after most of the pros had transitioned to three-fin thrusters. Like Cheyne Horan she could make them look good, but her surfing became more seamless when she started riding Greg Clough Aloha thrusters in 1985.

In 1989 Mark Rabbidge started making her boards, adding personal shaper to a list of roles that included, according to historian Matt Warshaw, 'technique and strategy coach, agent–manager, screening phone calls and booking plane tickets, car rentals, and hotel reservations'. Moreover, along with being her soulmate he was her lover. As Burridge recalled: 'I was starting to feel we had a little team going. Competing was finally starting to feel normal. I was getting feedback and I was in a relationship that I was happy with, and things just started to change. I opened up as a person. I was a lot more easy-going than I'd been. I was growing up, finally.'

> 'I had to work on a new approach to my contest surfing. I finally figured out that I didn't handle pressure well at all.'

In 1990 Pam teamed a run of high placings with two mid-season victories, and she went into the last event at Sunset Beach looking for her third world title and with a narrow lead over Wendy Botha. She recalled: 'About halfway through the 1990 season Mark and I were flying to California, with some good results already behind me, and I thought, "If I can win here, I can win the world championship."' She won the Women's Cup at Oceanside and went into the Hawaiian season with a narrow lead over Botha and in the box seat.

In double-overhead peaks at Sunset Beach for the Women's Hurley Pro, Pam looked relaxed and confident. This time it was Botha who stumbled in the first round, and after a decade of trying Pam Burridge was Australia's first women's world professional champion. She said later: 'I packed my boards away and went, "Thank you very much." It felt like I'd been a prisoner and I'd just been released with a full acquittal.'

Burridge and Rabbidge were married in 1993, and the following year they moved to Bendalong on the surf-rich New South Wales South Coast. She retired from the tour briefly but decided she wasn't quite ready to make babies in the bush, so she came back and finished third in 1997 before retiring for good the following year, with 20 tour wins to her credit. She'd been ranked in the top eight for 15 seasons.

Pam and Mark are still happily married and living the rural idyll in Bendalong with two grown children and three dogs. They are totally immersed in the surfing lifestyle, with Pam running two surf schools and women's surfing retreats and Mark shaping. Pam was inducted into the Sport Australia Hall of Fame in 1996 and the Australian Surfing Hall of Fame in 1997.

Doing what she loves: teaching groms at a South Coast beach. Photo courtesy Pam Burridge Surf School.

At Bells for the Women's Rip Curl Pro, 2009. Photo Joli.

10

LAYNE BEACHLEY

Full name	Layne Collette Beachley
Nickname	Gidget
Birthdate	24 May 1972
Place of birth	Sydney, New South Wales

The name is not her birth name, but had she adopted it as a stage name it could not have been more appropriate.

Layne Beachley has not one but two qualifications for entry into the admittedly subjective listing of Australia's surfing immortals. The first is her extraordinary run of seven world professional titles, six of them consecutive, which was an unbroken record until Steph Gilmore bettered it by winning her eighth world title in September 2022.

The second qualification is that no female surfer has come anywhere near her ability and courage in huge waves. Hawaii's Keala Kennelly may have come close, and in recent years of extreme surfing at newer locations such as Nazaré in Portugal surfers such as Brazil's Maya Gabeira may have towed into a bigger drop, but no woman so far in surfing history has matched Beachley's all-round ability and fearlessness in waves of extreme consequence.

Beachley's statistics alone are jaw dropping: seven world titles between 1998 and 2006; five event wins in a season three times; and 29 career world tour event victories. Throughout her career, however, she was always more than the sum of her parts – a sassy, opinionated, funny, ruthless, street-smart operator and savvy competitor and, above all, a remarkable ambassador for women's surfing. But it was no easy road to get there.

Layne was born prematurely as Tania Maris Gardner in Sydney on 24 May 1972 and put up for adoption soon after by her single mother. The circumstances of these events only became apparent to her many years later with devastating consequences, but as an eight-month-old baby she was fortunate to be adopted by Neil and Valerie Beachley, who renamed her Layne Collette Beachley, took her to their comfortable Balgowlah home and loved her as their own.

Living adjacent to Manly and Sydney's Northern Beaches peninsula, Neil Beachley was a keen beachgoer and introduced Layne at an early age to the lifestyle. She told biographer Michael Gordon: 'I started skateboarding when I was three, surfing when I was four, and was paddling out the back and surfing on my own when I was five.' The early start in surfing was soon diluted by her intense desire to be good at every sport she encountered, particularly after the sudden and unexpected death of Val Beachley during routine surgery. Layne was not even seven years of age, and as Mickey Gordon noted 'She had already lost two mothers.'

According to family friends who looked after Layne and her five-years-older stepbrother Jason while Neil was away working, the two fought like cats and dogs but

> 'I started skateboarding when I was three, surfing when I was four, and was paddling out the back and surfing on my own when I was five.'

shared a distaste for vegetables and showering. Layne was a tomboy through and through but she is remembered as a good kid, if a little reluctant to express affection. She was certainly determined to be the best at whatever activity was presented to her, except hygiene and a balanced diet.

Before Layne had started her secondary schooling at Mackellar Girls High, Neil retired from his travelling sales and marketing job to become a full-time dad, affording him the time to ferry her to her many sporting obligations. As short as she was, Layne tried basketball, water polo, tennis, cricket, hockey and athletics, but in the end the beach won out. By the time she was 14 she was a fixture at Manly Beach, known to all and sundry as 'Gidget' after the film and television California surf girl. She surfed before and after school and worked part time at Guy Leech and Doug Lees's Australian Surfer HQ shop.

On her way to winning the Roxy Pro Hawaii, 1999. Photo Joli.

In the pocket, Teahupo'o, Tahiti, 2000. Photo Joli.

As Sean Doherty put it in his 2020 book *Golden Daze*: 'Layne Beachley would skate along the beachfront at Manly like she owned the place. Dressed in teenage boys' surfwear, board under her arm, hat on backwards, she'd weave through the joggers and day-trippers along the Steyne with one eye ahead and one on the waves.'

Both Lees and Leech became mentors and sponsors at the start of Layne's career but it was Leech, the blond Adonis who had only recently won Australia's first professional ironman event, the Coolangatta Gold, who inspired her with his dedication to hard training and his profound one-liners. Decades later, when they'd both done a lot of time on the speakers' circuit, Layne credited Leech for getting her thinking about inspiring others.

Surfing was becoming her life, but beyond club comps with Queenscliff Boardriders she didn't compete until quite a late age, entering the regional scholastics event at Curl Curl in 1988 at the age of 16. She won it easily, and recalled years later:

> *Brimming with confidence, I then went on to represent at the NSW Scholastic Titles and won those too. I was on a roll! Later that year I experienced for the first time what being part of a 'team' could mean,*

> when I competed in the National Scholastics. This experience had a profound impact on me and influenced my decision to become a professional surfer. I never realised that 'mates' could be so vicious, relentless in their teasing, hurtful and mean-spirited. Admittedly, I learnt fairly quickly to give as good as I got, but these guys gave more than I could handle.

If she found the rough and tumble of amateur surfing hard to handle, how was she going to deal with the pro game? Layne later wrote:

> Of course, my lack of experience within the amateur ranks hindered my performance in the early pro tour years, but those challenges just made me work harder and become more resolute to make it to the top. Growing up on Sydney's northern beaches certainly had its advantages. World champions surrounded me. Surfing with Barton Lynch, Wendy Botha, Pam Burridge, Tom Carroll, Martin Potter and Midget Farrelly was a wonderful privilege. They were an encyclopedia of knowledge and experience, and I was a sponge. One of the best pieces of advice I was given, was to learn from the mistakes and experiences of others. All of these people had what I wanted and fortunately for me they were willing to share it.

Layne qualified for the pro tour after finishing school at the end of 1989, but success was not immediate. After competing in half of the tour events in 1990, she finished 17th in the rankings with only a third placing at Newcastle as a keeper. The next year wasn't much better, although she did move up the rankings to 12th. With 15 events on the schedule around the world in 1992, Layne spent a lot of money on airline tickets for not much return in the modest women's prize-money pool. In fact, it was a stinker of a season until the fourth-last event, the Miyazaki Pro in Japan.

On a roll, she claimed a second at the next event in Brazil and a third at the Marui Women's Masters in Hawaii. Although the Marui was held at Haleiwa and she didn't fare so well at the next event, the Hard Rock Café World Cup of Surfing in the big, shifting peaks of Sunset Beach, Layne felt she had made her mark on the North Shore, Oahu's epicentre of surfing, and she moved into the home season at the start of 1993 with new confidence.

After middling results in Newcastle, Margaret River and Bells Beach, Layne hit her home turf for the Diet Coke Surf Classic at North Narrabeen in the best shape she'd been in on tour. Over the past couple of seasons she had developed a support crew around her that included fitness trainer to the stars Rob Rowland-Smith, aka the 'Sandhill Warrior' for his punishing hill runs at Palm Beach. Rob was a growling, grizzled man whose face had seen a lot of sun and whose mullet needed a trim, but he was inspirational. Also in Layne's corner was Mark Rabbidge, the husband of 1990 world women's champion Pam Burridge and a longboard champion himself, who had identified and worked on some technical aspects of Layne's surfing along with shaping her boards.

She won the Diet Coke, the richest women's event on tour, from Kylie Webb in a tense final and claimed her first tour victory just two weeks short of her 21st birthday. To celebrate she bought an expensive training bike and, having reached her majority, decided it was time she moved out of Neil Beachley's home. She struck out on her own, renting a room from Tom and Lisa Carroll and also

Layne hit her home turf for the Diet Coke Surf Classic at North Narrabeen in the best shape she'd been in on tour.

taking on the role of babysitter to their two toddlers (a fairly short-lived gig!).

There was a cloud on the horizon in the form of a strange lethargy that overtook her in the weeks after her Narrabeen win. Layne cut back on training sessions with Rowland-Smith but the symptoms persisted, eventually leading to a diagnosis of chronic fatigue syndrome – a condition that continued to plague her through her early years on tour.

Layne finished her third full year on tour with a sixth-place ranking and with widespread and growing recognition that she was world champion material. Having never pulled any punches about that being her stated ambition, cheeky Layne might well have said: 'Well, duh!' However, 1994 turned out to be the breakthrough year for a Florida runaway named Lisa Andersen, who was a thorn in Layne's side for the next four years. Similar to Mark Richards's four-year stranglehold on the world title in the early 1980s and Kelly Slater's six titles in the 1990s, Andersen's dominance drove several of the women's contenders from the tour. Layne Beachley was never going to be one of them, and the rivalry between the two women became intense.

Beachley finished fourth behind Andersen in 1994, second in 1995, third in 1996 and second again in 1997. She began the 1998 circuit accompanied by veteran Hawaiian big-wave surfer Ken Bradshaw, 19 years her senior, who over the North Shore winter had become her boyfriend, coach, board shaper and big-wave mentor. Layne dominated the schedule, winning five of 11 events – Bells, Manly, Japan, Huntington Beach and

At age 39 Layne led the Australian team to victory (and another personal world title) at the ISA World Masters, Peru, 2011. Photo ISA.

Hossegor, France – on her way to a comprehensive world title victory.

Layne's elevation to world number one at last was a landmark in her career in two ways. First, early in the 1998 season Lisa Andersen pulled out of competition to nurse a recurring back injury that kept her out of contention for the rest of the year and for the whole of 1999. She returned to competition sporadically thereafter in the early years of the new century but never challenged Beachley for the title.

With men's champion Kelly Slater retiring after wrestling his sixth

A playful off-the-top at the Noosa Festival of Surfing, 2014. Photo NFS.

world title from the two Aussies who seemed to have a stranglehold on it, the period of American dominance of the Association of Surfing Professionals (ASP) world tour had ended. It opened up an opportunity for Australia to rise again, particularly in 1999 after Layne won her second world title with another five event wins and Australia's Mark Occhilupo won the men's.

The second way that Layne's elevation to world number one was a landmark was because it marked the beginning of an all-encompassing relationship with Ken Bradshaw that would help define her as a surfer at the peak of her ability. Although they had been casual acquaintances over a couple of North Shore winters, it was only when Layne arrived in Hawaii in November 1997 and discovered that Bradshaw and his partner had split that it developed into the kind of relationship that is the stuff of romantic novels. However, it was only one level of it, as she was drawn into what sportswriter Bruce Jenkins called 'The Nation of Ken'.

A square-jawed jock from Texas who had been a fixture on the North Shore since the 1970s, when he became famous as a fast-improving big-wave rider with a hot temper in crowded surf, Bradshaw swept Layne off her feet. As Jenkins observed in the aforementioned article in *The Surfer's Journal* in 2000:

You see them on the beach, or in a restaurant, and it seems almost too good to be true: Bradshaw, the man who rode the biggest wave. Beachley, the three-time world champ and the all-time greatest female big-wave rider. On top of that, they are ridiculously in love. They wake up stoked and pursue the sport of surfing together, all day long. It wouldn't occur to them to be apart for any reason, save the occasional demands of travel.

This is a love affair so intense, it has shifted Bradshaw's focus away from his own career. Not that he's over it – he's still looking for an even bigger wave to ride – but he channels his energy into Layne now: her career, her tow-in passion, and the tenuous mental edge she holds over her competition. It seems likely that Beachley would have taken the women's throne on her own, such is the calibre of her talent and resolve. But Bradshaw's presence gives her a mighty,

> *almost unbeatable look. It is a presence she desperately needs.*

However, as Layne's biographer Michael Gordon noted, the nation of Ken was 'a territory ruled by the power of waves, where daily routines, travel schedules and goals are dictated by weather patterns, swell size and direction. From the beginning, Ken . . . was the dominant partner.'

There were several downsides to this, but one of them was not Bradshaw's contribution to Layne's surfing development. A couple of weeks after they became lovers he taught her to tow into big waves at Outside Log Cabins. That winter she won her first Hawaiian Triple Crown, a feat she repeated in her title year of 1998. As surf historian Matt Warshaw noted:

> *Beachley's competitive success was paralleled by her development as a big-wave rider. She'd performed well in the powerful Hawaiian surf through the early and mid-'90s, but in late 1997, as her relationship with Bradshaw took off, she surpassed all the female big-wave benchmarks set years earlier by the likes of Hawaii's Margo Oberg and Australian Jodie Cooper.*

> *On 22 December 1997, with Bradshaw driving the jet-ski, Beachley was catapulted into a handful of 20-foot waves at a North Shore break called Phantoms. Sarah Gerhardt of California had earlier become the first woman tow-in surfer, but Beachley was the first woman to master the art. She later towed in to 25-footers at Outside Log Cabins and Todos Santos in Baja California, and was the first woman to ride terrifying slab barrels at Ours, in Sydney.* Outside *magazine in 1998 published a profile on Beachley titled 'I'm Going Big. Anyone Care to Follow?'*

Ken Bradshaw was never far from Layne's side as she continued her relentless gathering of ornaments for the trophy room. Considerably incapacitated by a knee injury during the 1999 season, she still managed to win four of the season's 14 events and a second world title. *Surfer* magazine described her as 'simply the most powerful woman in surfing today'. For her 2000 title she won four of nine, then she won one of the three events in the 9/11–abbreviated 2001 season. In 2002 she won just one of six contests, but it was enough to

Fearless in waves of consequence: Layne at Sunset Beach, 1999. Photo Joli.

earn the title and make her the only five-time women's tour champion. In 2003 she won just one of five events and took the championship again but her hot run was over, as was her relationship with Bradshaw.

Layne had become increasingly exhausted by her partner's incessant questioning of her training and performances and his attempted manipulation of her schedule. It blew up in France in August 2002 when Layne, looking to make history with a fifth world title, had not yet won an event. Her dream was going up in smoke and all Ken could do was huff and puff. With the Quiksilver Pro Hossegor about to begin and Ken's 50th birthday just a few days away, she told him it was over.

Bradshaw was devastated, but he took it like the big tough Texan he was. He stayed to watch her win the contest and lead the rankings into the next, her world title aims back on track. She organised a birthday party for him before they left Hossegor. It seemed amicable enough, that they could remain friends, but of course it wasn't quite over and it got quite messy.

Bradshaw was still in her corner when the tour moved to Hawaii and still offering sound advice while he tried to win her back. The girl was not for turning, and when she secured her fifth world title in Maui she flew back to Australia – where the man who would share the next chapter of her life was waiting.

Having won six world titles Layne now had seven in her sights, but 2004 was not to be her year and she slipped back to fourth in the rankings. The following year was even worse. Plagued by injuries throughout, she was nevertheless an outside chance for a title going into the Hawaiian season but a training ride on her bike went horribly wrong and landed her in hospital and out of the last two events.

While she seemed to be losing her winning way in the water, Beachley was developing an enviable but dangerously high profile in the surf industry. Having left her first major sponsor Quiksilver for rival Billabong, she found herself frequently at odds with management over her outspoken comments on women's rights both in the industry and the professional sport. As the women surfers' representative on the ASP she was constantly on the front foot, pushing for equal prize money and better conditions. The highest profile surfer in Australia and, excluding Kelly Slater, in the world, she knew she had the power to influence people but she didn't want to do that as a corporate mouthpiece.

Layne left Billabong and went out on her own, establishing the Beachley brand and the Beachley Surf Classic, which debuted at Manly in 2006 just in time to see Layne make her run at the title. She lost the final to a wildcard named Steph Gilmore, but second was enough to

Hall of Fame induction, 2000. Photo Joli.

With fellow GOAT Kelly Slater at the ASP awards banquet, 2012. Photo Joli.

put her at the top of the rankings and she went on to win her seventh and last ASP world title.

At the age of 34 Beachley still had plenty to give to surfing, but she also had a new life to build with partner Kirk Pengilly, the brilliant multi-instrumentalist of INXS fame. When the two had started dating in late 2002 Layne explained that 'opposites attract'. While it was true that the dapper rock star never looked terribly comfortable with sand between his toes, he soon became very popular throughout the surfing world for his humour, generosity of spirit and abiding love for Layne. The couple married in 2010.

Towards the end of her pro surfing career Layne reconciled with her birth mother Maggie and her family, having discovered that she had been born as the result of a date rape. It's been a sometimes difficult relationship but it has helped Layne focus more on women's issues in her post-surfing careers in media, mentoring and motivational public speaking. She is also the founder and director of her own charitable foundation, Aim for the Stars, chairperson of Surfing Australia and an Officer of the Order of Australia. She was inducted into the Australian Surfing Hall of Fame in 2006.

Layne and Kirk live in a hillside house with a view of the ocean at Freshwater Beach, where she still shows the boys a thing or two whenever there's a swell.

Steph smashes a lip at the Rip Curl Search, Puerto Rico, 2010. Photo Joli.

11

STEPH GILMORE

Full name	Stephanie Louise Gilmore
Nickname	Steph, Happy Gilmore
Birthdate	29 January 1988
Place of birth	Murwillumbah, New South Wales

Fifteen years after winning her first world title, in 2022 Steph Gilmore won her eighth, eclipsing Layne Beachley as the greatest of all time . . . and she's not done yet.

Sometimes – too often, in fact – bad things happen to good people for no discernible reason.

Having secured her fourth consecutive world title in Hawaii early in December 2010, Stephanie Gilmore had flown home for Christmas to spend it with family and friends. The day after Boxing Day she had been visiting friends nearby and might have walked had not the rain come in that afternoon, so she drove. After dinner she returned to her Coolangatta apartment, parked her car in the ground-floor lot and began walking toward the stairs. Journalist Sean Doherty takes up the story:

She sensed she wasn't alone. From the shadows a figure ran at her and struck her with what turned out to be a metal bar. She turned as he swung again, blocking the next strike with her left arm. She screamed and the guy took off on a pushbike. The attacker would turn out to be a homeless guy, a schizophrenic who'd never met Steph. He didn't even know Steph was Steph. It was shitty luck sent from the wider cosmos.

Shielding the second blow earned Steph a broken wrist and she had scalp wounds that required stitches, relatively minor injuries considering what might have been, and she was back in the water in a couple of weeks. The psychological wounds took longer to heal.

Six months after the attack Doherty was with Steph and a group of friends, including her surfboard shaper Darren Handley and legendary shaper Simon Anderson, on a Mentawai Islands surf charter. He later wrote:

> *No one on board was sure exactly how Steph was coping. Nobody broached the subject of 'the night'. She offered the story after dinner one evening, unprompted. She recounted the details slowly, deliberately. She asked questions of the night, questions of the days after, questions to herself. It was clearly still lurking there and she was obviously still processing large parts of it. For someone of Steph's sunny disposition and good fortune, these were uncharted waters.*

That's it, right there. Steph had become the golden girl of world surfing almost overnight, winning the world title in her rookie year on tour and going on to make it four successive titles, but what had endeared her to the Australian public even more than her incredible ability and natural flowing style was her 'sunny disposition'. She was 'Happy' Gilmore, almost never seen without a broad smile on her face, bending down her lithe, willowy frame to sign autographs for legions of tiny fans as she made her way up from the surf after a heat, never flustered and never boastful in her media appearances but making her important points – often about equal prize money for women – concisely and authoritatively. In surfing, in most sports, ambassadors don't come any better.

Then some deranged man attacked her with an iron bar. It was unfathomable.

A personal aside: in early September 2010, not quite three months before the attack, I was way back in the economy check-in queue for the Virgin flight to Los Angeles when I noticed Steph – yes, the economy line even with three world titles, soon to be four – further towards the front standing tall in a sea of people. She was somewhat preoccupied with texting, but rose to the occasion with every request for an autograph or selfie. She didn't know me well but waved enthusiastically when she spied me. I noted that she never let a fan down throughout her extended wait; in her entire career she rarely has.

In the zone: Hawaii, 2010. Photo Joli.

Born Stephanie Louise Gilmore in 1988 in what was then the sleepy fishing town of Kingscliff, New South Wales, just over the border and 20 minutes down the highway from the Snapper Rocks Superbank, to parents she has described as 'a little bit hippie', Steph grew up on the beach and was riding a bodyboard as well as most of the boys at the age of nine. A year later she had progressed to a surfboard. The youngest of three girls, she was as she told writer Tim Baker 'a tomboy, the son they never had'. Always happy to get a laugh at her own expense, Steph told another interviewer: 'I didn't shave my legs until I was, like, 16.'

Jeff and Tracy Gilmore were both surf people, Jeff a passionately committed surfer of whom Steph told *Vogue Australia*: 'Seeing my dad be so passionate about it, that is what really ingrained in me how special surfing is, and that is what made me fall in love with it.'

Obviously Mum and Dad were going to do nothing to dissuade

her from surfing, driving her up the coast to Snapper Rocks before or after school. There she fell under the spell of the Coolie Kids Mick Fanning, Joel Parkinson and Dean Morrison, the kings of the superbank. Steph watched and learned. She joined the Snapper Rocks Surfriders Club and was soon at ease competing and free surfing in the perfect sand cylinders of the Gold Coast points.

Gilmore had begun making waves long before she turned pro, winning the New South Wales junior title in 2003 and really turning up the heat the next year when aged 16, winning the Australian junior title and the International Surfing Association world juniors in Tahiti.

Steph power slash, Rip Curl Pro, Bells Beach, 2017. Photo Joli.

Billabong Pipe Masters, 2010. Photo Joli.

Still at school, she was now on the world stage. At the end of 2004 Rip Curl, always quick to spot emerging talent, signed her to a lucrative five-year sponsorship deal. valued at more than $1,000,000 subject to her turning pro and qualifying for the world tour.

Soon after signing the deal she was offered a wildcard entry into the Roxy Pro at her home break of Snapper Rocks. She approached it with the confidence of a 17 year old with nothing to lose, beat superstar multiple world champion Layne Beachley by a micro point in the semi-finals in perfect surf then

At the end of 2004 Rip Curl, always quick to spot emerging talent, signed her to a lucrative five-year sponsorship deal.

crushed Hawaiian Megan Abubo in the final with a 9.33 winning ride to take the $20,000 prize money. There was already a buzz about Happy Gilmore, but after the Roxy win against the best surfers in the world it became a roar. Not only did Steph have the flowing style and natural ability of a born champion, she had a wonderfully exuberant spirit and

Steph Gilmore · 151

sense of fun. Right from the start she was a marketing dream. '"Million dollar baby" Stephanie Gilmore is taking aim at a trailblazing route to surfing stardom,' *The Sydney Morning Herald* noted in a rather mixed up article later that year.

> *Just two weeks after fellow Snapper Rocks surfer Chelsea Georgeson won the women's world title, recent year 12 graduate Gilmore is boldly hoping to do the same one day, and perhaps surpass Layne Beachley's record six titles. 'To be successful and make enough money to be set-up in my life – and maybe a world title [win] or seven along the way,' Gilmore declares about her career ambition. Cocky perhaps, but when you see what this northern NSW teenager has done in 2005 you won't think so.*

More prescient than cocky, with Gilmore going on to do just that. She had certainly had an extraordinary year, right down to sitting for her final exams at the Australian consulate in Los Angeles en route to the World Surfing Games.

With school behind her, Steph hit the road on the qualifying series in 2006 and was sitting pretty for world-tour qualification at number two in the rankings when she was given another wildcard, this time for the Havaianas Beachley Classic at Manly. Again, she had nothing to lose and surfed methodically through the rounds until meeting Beachley in the final. Layne, surfing at her home beach in the contest she had started, had racked up a nine in her semi-final to defeat reigning world champion Chelsea Georgeson. Having been beaten by the upstart Gilmore grom in the Roxy Pro the year before, she had her winner's face on this time.

However, it was not to be. Steph got in early with two good rides and Beachley was never in the lead. It was an emphatic victory and Gilmore, who had made the record books in 2005 as the youngest woman to have won an Association of Surfing Professionals world tour event, did so again, this time as the first woman to have won two events as a wildcard.

As a tour rookie in 2007 Gilmore made it look too easy, cruising to her first world title by winning four of eight events, including another Beachley Classic and the Rip Curl Pro at Bells Beach. This cemented her popularity with the Australian public and delighted her major sponsor, even as they realised the teenager was swiftly moving towards her bonused million-dollar promise. Steph had gone to the top of the rankings after winning at Bells early in the season but then faltered slightly at the end, taking it to the early rounds of the final event at Honolua Bay before the title was hers. The bay became a happy hunting ground for her over the years.

In yet another entry in the record books, Gilmore became the first rookie – man or woman – to win the championship tour.

Defending her title in 2008, Steph notched up five wins from seven events, including both of the Hawaiian events. In 2009 things were a little tighter, with only one victory in the Roxy Pro at Snapper

Taking a punt at Rocky Point, Hawaii, 2010. Photo Joli.

Steph claims her fourth world title in Puerto Rico, 2010. Photo Joli.

Rocks when the tour went into its final leg in Hawaii. She had a string of second placings to keep her in contention, but at the Gidget Pro Sunset Beach another five surfers also had a shot at the title. While Steph calmly navigated her way to the semis the other contenders were eliminated one by one, leaving her to surf her favoured Honolua Bay in the last event with no real pressure. She won it, of course.

Gilmore's fourth title campaign got off to a flyer with wins on the Gold Coast and at Bells, and she secured it at the Rip Curl Search event in Puerto Rico in early November 2010. Unfortunately, her celebrations were cut short when word of the tragic death of three-time world champion Andy Irons reached the pro camp just hours later. Irons had mysteriously withdrawn from the Puerto Rico event during the early men's rounds and was reportedly on his way back to Hawaii. He only got as far as Dallas, where he was found dead in an airport hotel room. The shadow of Irons's death at just 32 after years of reported drug abuse hung over the final leg of the tour in Hawaii, but Steph managed to stay positive by playing a guitar and shooting videos when not in the surf.

Then she flew home for Christmas and her own nightmare.

Although her physical wounds healed within a couple of weeks of the December 2010 attack, no one then knew the extent of the trauma she had suffered. It therefore came as a shock to the surfing world when Gilmore emerged on 5 January 2011, all smiles and vivacity, to announce that she had signed a $5,000,000, five-year deal to become the global brand ambassador for Quiksilver Women's, making her surfing's first million-dollar female pro. In surfing's small world changing camps to join a rival is never easy, but Steph made it look so.

'In my eyes,' she told a reporter at the announcement press conference, 'the best female surfer is someone who pulls into big barrels and can take getting scraped on the reef, but can then turn around and be graceful and stylish in beautiful waves in the most feminine way possible. That's what I'm trying to achieve.' Meanwhile, a new year had begun and she had world title number five in her sights.

Steph never quite found her rhythm in 2011 and finished third

> **Although her physical wounds healed within a couple of weeks of the attack, no one then knew the extent of the trauma she had suffered.**

in a year that established the career of 19-year-old Carissa Moore, the Hawaiian former prodigy who won her first championship title as easily as Steph had done. Layne Beachley, whose own record run of titles was stopped by Gilmore in 2007, told *Surfer* magazine that 'It was only a matter of time before the girls realised that they have the ability to not only beat Steph but to challenge her for a world title.' Maybe so, but don't poke the bear no matter how happy it looks. Gilmore bounced back in 2012, winning events on the Gold Coast, New Zealand and France to secure her fifth world title before the last contest of the year was held.

If 2011 had been a tough year overcoming trauma, albeit slightly softened by the million a year dropping into her account, 2013 was Gilmore's *annus horribilis*. Plagued by recurring injuries, she failed to win an event throughout the season in her worst showing as a pro and finished fifth in the rankings.

She also had to contend, for the first time in her career, with a negative media backlash. to a promotional video she did for the Roxy Pro Biarritz that showed her not surfing but getting out of bed and putting on a negligee to some chill beats. It was sexy in a sweet way but by no means offensive. Not having seen this coming, Roxy ran for cover while Steph left it to dad Jeff to explain that if it got more people interested in women's surfing then it was a good thing. Strangely, the critics of the Roxy promo had been silent in 2011 when Gilmore posed for the cover of the body issue of *ESPN* magazine, possibly because Kelly Slater had done the same the previous year.

In 2014 Gilmore won three events for the season – on the Gold Coast, where she sat in with Jimmy Buffet for an impromptu concert on a lay day at Snapper, at Trestles and Cascais, Portugal – taking it down to the last contest of the year, the Target Maui Pro Women's at Honolua Bay, where her fifth-place finish was just enough to earn her a sixth world title. Commentator Chris Cote wrote of the drama of that day: 'In the dying minutes of the final heat of the Maui Pro, Stephanie Gilmore held her breath while

> **She also had to contend, for the first time in her career, with a negative media backlash.**

Carissa Moore surfed an incredible heat, knocking Tyler Wright out of world title contention, and cementing Gilmore's name in the annals of surf history by giving her a sixth world title.'

Then came the dog days, when it appeared that the world title game of pass the parcel between Steph and Carissa Moore had ended. Beset by injuries again, Steph didn't win an event in 2015 (finishing 12th) or 2016 (sixth), but the numbers were at least heading north again. After winning her two home events at Snapper Rocks and Honolua Bay to finish second in 2017, Gilmore felt renewed and buoyed to go after her next target: to catch up to Layne again.

In 2018 she won at Bells Beach and in Rio, and it was enough to give her a seventh world title. The remarkable rivalry between Australia's two record-breaking surf champions entered its final phase, with Beachley retired and powerless to improve her title count and Gilmore, then aged 30, finding it harder every year to keep up with

At the ASP awards night, Gold Coast, 2013. Photo Joli.

the emerging talent. Which is not to say she was about to throw the towel in: far from it.

In the 10-event 2019 season she won in Bali and at Honolua Bay to finish in fourth place, the highest-ranked Australian on the women's tour, when along came the COVID-19 intervention, which cancelled the tour in 2020. In the abbreviated, on-and-off 2021 tour Steph finished second at Margaret River and won the final event in Mexico to finish fifth overall. She also won selection to represent her country at that year's delayed Tokyo Olympics but was eliminated early and had to simply cheer on teammate Owen Wright to a bronze medal, while Carissa Moore took the women's gold.

If ever a season could be considered career-defining, Stephanie Gilmore's 2022 would be it. No matter how much longer she stays on the pro tour, the highs, the lows, the sheer drama of it are unlikely to be surpassed.

To kick it off, a positive COVID-19 test just before the historic return of the women's event to the Pipeline saw her eliminated from the contest with minimum points when it began the day before her Covid protocol of seven days isolation finished.

It was a crushing blow, and after a moderate showing at the next event at Sunset Beach, she had to 'crawl my way back into the cut', meaning the ruthless mid-season culling of almost half the field. But Steph fired back with third placings in Portugal and at Jeffrey's Bay, and a victory in El Savador enabled her to scrape into the last position in the final five.

The win against California's Lakey Peterson in tricky conditions in El Salvador was a classic Gilmore buzzer beater. With 11 minutes remaining in the 40-minute final she had 1.03 points against her name to Peterson's 9.67. With even modest scores hard to come by, Steph found a 7.33 and backed it up ahead of the buzzer with a 5.67 to claim the victory.

Carving at Sunset Beach in the Gidget Pro, Hawaii, 2009. Photo Joli.

She said later: 'I would love to win another world title, but it's still a long road.'

That road ended across the railroad tracks at Lower Trestles, California on 8 September 2022. In the second year of the WSL's 'final five' knockout format, Steph was at very long odds to take an historic eighth world title, having to beat everyone else in the five by surfing a minimum of five heats in one gruelling day. In conditions that suited her style of surfing, she still looked nervous and off her rhythm in the first heat against Costa Rica's Brisa Hennessy, but managed a comeback with a combination of good scores.

From this point on there was no stopping Gilmore. Growing in confidence, she dispatched Brazil's Tatiana Weston-Webb and France's Johanne Defay before meeting the favourite, world number one and reigning 2021 champion, Hawaii's Carissa Moore, in the best-of-three-sets grand final. Despite the fact that she had already surfed three 35-minute heats, Gilmore looked energetic and in career-best form. She crushed the Hawaiian in straight sets.

As the final hooter announced that with her eighth title she had officially pulled ahead of Layne Beachley as the greatest female surfer of all time, Steph paddled over to the WSL water reporter, grabbed his microphone and in typical Aussie fashion, let out a roaring crow call to share her joy with viewers around the world.

Despite a magnitude of competing interests in her life, Happy Gilmore's sponsors have always loved her. A decade since signing her first million-dollar a year contract with Roxy, she remains the leading brand ambassador. And in late 2018 she also signed a long-term deal to become the global face of Audi, the German car brand that best fit her growing eco-awareness. Her first public appearance for the brand was at the San Francisco launch of Audi's E-Tron electric vehicle.

Gilmore had also used her international profile to advocate for ocean conservation for some years, but in 2018 she added pay parity for women's pro surfers to her list of causes. In September of that year the world's two highest profile surfers, Kelly Slater and Stephanie Gilmore, released a joint statement in support of the World Surf League's ground-breaking announcement of equal prize money for women and men on the professional circuit.

Wright on a rail, Bells Beach, 2012. Photo Joli.

TYLER WRIGHT

Full name	Tyler Grace Wright
Nickname	Ty
Birthdate	31 March 1994
Place of birth	Culburra, New South Wales

Marching to the beat of her own drum, Tyler Wright has won two world titles and inspired a generation of surfers.

The tricky pathway endured by sporting child prodigies is not uncommon, but in the case of two-time world champion Tyler Wright, who became the youngest winner of a world title event in history in 2008 when aged 14, the World Surf League (WSL) tagline of 'You can't script this' was never more appropriate.

Seemingly on top of the world in early 2018 after winning her second successive world title and thrilled to see her big brother Owen back on tour after a life-threatening brain injury, by mid-year the power surfer from the New South Wales South Coast was suddenly faced with a series of events that shattered her health, drained her bank account and made her doubt who she really was and what she wanted in life.

However, the Wright we've watched grow up in the surf over the past 15 years does not give up. If a section shuts her down she foam climbs over it or works her way under it and resumes her attack on the wave with renewed zeal. That's what she's still doing as she fights her way back into contention for a third world title and as she fights for recognition of the real Tyler Wright.

The fourth of five children, Tyler was born to mother Fiona and father Rob at Culburra Beach, near the rural centre of Nowra, in 1994. The whole family was surf mad but brother Owen, four years Tyler's senior, showed the most talent early on. By the time Tyler was five, however, Rob Wright realised she no longer needed his push into waves, and having caught one by herself she knew what to do with it. She began surfing with her siblings Tim, Owen, Kirby and, when he came along, Mikey, and a group of about 15 other kids who lived in the small network of streets near their house opposite the beach.

Owen Wright recalled in a joint ESPN interview with Tyler in 2012 that he and older brother Tim started surfing with their dad, but 'as I got older and the family bigger, we would surf together with a bunch of other local crew pushing each other to do bigger turns, sit deeper on the bank and generally charge as hard as we could when the waves got bigger.'

Tyler chimed in: 'Being younger, I just tagged along and tried to do what my brothers and sister [Kirby] were doing . . . but better [laughs]. It was all about having fun for me. When I'm out surfing it's like having six coaches in the water, they all have their opinions on everything and they all think they're right 99.9 percent of the time. I love it.'

Asked about what kind of role model father Rob Wright had been as a surfer, Owen responded: 'We didn't have coaches on the South

> By the time Tyler was five, Rob Wright realised she no longer needed his push into waves, and having caught one by herself she knew what to do with it.

Coast, so we worked with what resources we had. Dad is the biggest grom in the house, he's up early every day ready and checking the waves. He's going out anyway, I pretty much owe my love of surfing to [D]ad, he introduced me to surfing when I was about five and made sure we were hooked and able to coach ourselves.
I haven't looked back.'

Tyler said: 'Yeah, Dad's been a massive influence on getting me addicted to surfing, I don't think it was too hard for him 'cause once we were into it we never looked back and neither did he. We went on some of the most epic road trips ever and he taught us the true meaning of roughing it.'

Interviewer: 'Did your old man ever sit you down and talk about world titles?'

Tyler: 'That would be equivalent to him sitting us down and having

Proudly taking a knee at the Tweed Coast Pro, 2020. Photo Surfing Australia.

the sex talk, one of those things that's just not in his nature [laughs].'

Owen: 'Yeah, he's not that type. Dad never talked to me about world titles. He was always talking about having fun doing what you love, while using your head. I was the one chasing him for information, the support was there.'

It sounds like idyllic family fun, but as both Owen and Tyler became earmarked as champions of the future the pressure began to intensify. For one thing, there was no room for being a little kid. 'I got smashed so many times,' Tyler told ESPN. She then related the story of one incident where she 'popped up, grabbed a breath and disappeared under the surf, where I lost awareness of my board until a fin strikes me in the head. I got stitches in my forehead,' Wright said, rubbing the spot with her fingers.

She was back in the water the next day. 'She never cried,' mum Fiona told ESPN. In the Wright household toughness was currency, especially with dad Rob, a surfer whose passion for the sport was at the core of his existence and for which everything else had to fit around it. 'We were raised to push through everything,' Wright's sister Kirby told ESPN.

'Even if you had a severe injury, it wasn't made to be a big deal. Get stitched up and let's go for a surf.'

While all the Wright kids could surf, everyone could see that Owen and Tyler had something special and that little Mikey was developing it. Rob invested in a six-bed campervan so he could drive the kids around the circuit of amateur events. When Owen was aged 12 and Tyler just eight both were picked up for the Rip Curl junior sponsorship program, beginning a relationship with the brand that continues today. At 12, Tyler started getting cash payments as well as clothes and equipment.

Tyler had already established herself as a leading light in amateur junior events, but she really exploded into the limelight in 2008 as a 14 year old when she gained a wildcard entry into the Beachley Classic in Sydney. She took out world champion Steph Gilmore – her mentor at Rip Curl – on her way to winning the contest and became the youngest ever winner of an Association of Surfing Professionals (ASP) world tour event. The poise and style she showed during a hard-fought final against Brazil's Silvana Lima was way beyond her years, but her true age emerged when she was asked by an interviewer how she had celebrated her victory:

> **[Tyler] exploded into the limelight in 2008 as a 14 year old when she gained a wildcard entry into the Beachley Classic in Sydney.**

'I went home and cleaned my room and then I went to bed,' she said.

The impact on Tyler of a whole new world of media attention was not lost on Beachley Classic founder Layne Beachley, who later told *60 Minutes*: 'I felt like I kind of threw her under the bus a little, because I invited her to the richest event in the world, handed a 14-year-old twenty grand and sent her back to high school. I don't think we really prepared her for the media onslaught that was going to follow.'

With both his star kids about to burst into the professional ranks, Rob made the shock decision to move the family to Lennox Head on the Far North Coast of New South Wales, one of his favourite breaks as a young surfer but also conveniently adjacent to the Tweed Coast – where Surfing Australia was about to start building a high-performance centre for emerging elite surfers and just across the border from sponsorland in West Burleigh, where most of the major companies had headquarters.

Here they were with the best waves and the best opportunities, except that, as Tyler later protested, nobody had asked her what she wanted. She felt lost at Lennox and pined for Culburra: not that she was anywhere much except on the road.

In 2009 the Wright family camper made its way around the coastline to the events, and while the year really belonged to Owen – who never lost a heat in winning the Australasian Pro Junior Series, became the world pro junior champion and qualified for the 2010 world tour – Tyler represented her country at the International Surfing Association World Juniors in Ecuador and won the women's individual title. With Owen about to join the world tour, Tyler and her family made the decision that she would leave school and join both the pro junior and the World Surf League Qualifying Series (QS) qualifying tours.

First pro surfer payday at 14 years old! With Layne Beachley at the Beachley Classic, Manly 2008. Photo Newspix.

Throwing spray at the Roxy Pro, Gold Coast, 2012. Photo Joli.

In October she took out the first leg of the junior series, winning the Oakley World Pro Junior in Bali. She then went to Hawaii for the first time and capped a fantastic debut season on the QS with a victory at the O'Neill World Cup at Sunset Beach, motoring past fellow Aussies Sally Fitzgibbons and Stephanie Gilmore and Hawaii's Coco Ho to take the final in sizeable waves.

The win at Sunset secured her place on the 2011 ASP World Tour but Tyler's season was far from over, with the Women's Triple Crown to be decided at Pipeline in a one-heat duel for the crown. Tyler had already acquitted herself well at Sunset and Haleiwa and in free-surfing at Rocky Point, but this was a step further for the 16 year old: battling it out against the best female surfers in the world in the most dangerous wave in the world for the first time.

Pitted against Steph Gilmore and Hawaii's Coco Ho and Alana Blanchard in a growing swell, Tyler was consistent through the first half and held the lead until Steph took off on a bomb. As the clock wound down a monster set approached. Tyler spun around for the first wave with mere seconds on the clock and got to her feet a split second outside the buzzer. Steph took the triple crown but Tyler won the rookie award. Far from disappointed, she told reporters the heat had been the highlight of her career so far.

She *was* disappointed, however, two weeks later back in Australia when her mentor, friend and rival Steph Gilmore parted company with Rip Curl to join Roxy just as Tyler signed on for a lucrative five-year contract. She had looked forward to sharing ambassadorial duties with Australia's most popular surfer, but now she was going to replace her.

On the eve of beginning her rookie year on the championship tour as the youngest qualifier ever, Wright should have felt an excitement borne of belief in her proven ability to win but, in fact, her self-belief was heading south. Part of that was the weight of the huge expectations of the public and the media. When Owen won rookie of the year after the 2010 season, the siblings' story grew new legs. Could we see an Australian brother and sister take out world titles in the same year?

The other part was that Rob Wright chose the moment to step away from his plumbing company to travel the world with Tyler, acting as both coach and manager. As Tyler later told ESPN in the most frank and revealing interview of her career: 'It is a privileged position to travel the world as a professional athlete. Everyone was

Could we see an Australian brother and sister take out world titles in the same year?

like, "You're living the dream at 16." I was like, "Whose dream? I don't f—ing dream of this s—. I want to read books. I want to go to school."'

On tour Tyler kept her negative thoughts to herself, but they didn't go away. 'I had so many thoughts at 16, but no language to articulate any of it,' she told ESPN. 'My environment on tour and at home was geared for me to not get educated, to not be vocal on any issues. Surfers are supposed to be smiling and grateful. I had no examples of women showing anger. But I was angry all the f—ing time.'

Nevertheless, when the tour opened on the Gold Coast in February Wright produced sensational form to cruise through the early rounds of the Roxy Pro, and in an electrifying final she finished runner-up to Hawaii's Carissa Moore. She backed this up with a third at the Subaru Pro in New Zealand to finish in fourth place on the rankings, winning the rookie of the year award at a canter. In 2012 she finished third in all three Australian events before taking her first victory as a tour competitor at the Roxy Pro France, again finishing fourth on the rankings. Clearly, winning a world title wasn't as easy as it had seemed.

Wright and Carissa Moore battled head to head throughout the 2013 season. Wright started off with a win at the season-opening Roxy Pro, and Moore answered back by taking both the Margaret River and Rip Curl pros. Wright pulled ahead two stops later with a win in Rio, then Moore won the next event. It all came down to the final contest of the season, the Cascais Pro in Portugal. In sloppy beach break waves Wright lost in the quarters, while Moore went on to win both the event and the 2013 title.

Tyler was getting closer, but her frustration was growing following another second-place finish in 2014 after picking up two wins and three seconds. She slumped to fifth position in 2015 and even pondered walking away at the age of 19. Meanwhile, relations with her father had worsened. She told Rob that to remain on tour she needed a support system, not a manager. She stated on ESPN: 'I said, "You've got a choice. You're my dad or my manager." He said, "I'm your manager."'

During that difficult 2015 season Wright's parents divorced, Rob left the tour and 20-year-old Kirby became chaperone and support person. 'What I needed as a human wasn't what my dad was willing to give,' Wright told ESPN. 'Kirby knew that I wasn't healthy emotionally, and she got me to start to share what I was feeling.'

Towards the end of the season something clicked. After a close loss to Carissa Moore at Trestles, Tyler found herself caring again. 'I was like, "This is what it feels like to care,"' she told ESPN. 'I even gave myself permission to say it out loud: "I want to win a world title."' She underlined that with her only win of the season in France.

Two days before the 2015 men's season-ending Pipeline Masters, Tyler and Owen Wright enjoyed a leisurely breakfast with surf writer Sean Doherty at Café Haleiwa on the North Shore. The siblings were playful and full of jokes about the kind of year they'd both had. Owen had won in perfect waves in Fiji but had spent more time chasing giant swells than focusing on the tour. However, he was still in contention going into Pipe. Doherty later wrote: 'With a mouthful of food Owen joked that his catchphrase all year had been, "I just feel a little . . . different."'

At the O'Neill World Cup, Hawaii, 2010. Photo Joli.

The next morning during a warm-up session at Pipe, Owen was caught underneath a Second Reef set and washed all the way to the beach in a daze. He walked back to the house, ate, slept, then tried to get up. He couldn't. Tyler told Doherty: 'When they were loading Owen into the ambulance I was standing there watching, not outwardly freaking but looking into my brother's eyes and thinking, he's not there.'

It was a life-changing day for both siblings: for Owen the beginning of a long fight back from serious brain injury that he almost didn't make, and for Tyler the realisation of how much her brother meant to her and the dilemma of deciding whether to be a carer or a world-title contender.

With Owen still undergoing tests and treatment to determine his immediate future, Tyler went into the season-opening Roxy Pro at Snapper Rocks 'underdone and overwhelmed'. Nevertheless, she found inner strength and won the event.

As Doherty wrote: 'Brothers Tim and Mikey Wright carried her up the beach into the surfers' area and straight into the arms of Owen, who'd flown up to surprise her. He looked washed out and spectral, but Owen wouldn't have been anywhere else. That embrace crystallised Tyler's year. She'd been torn. In the end Owen made the choice for her. He said: "Go."' After further victories at Margaret River and Rio, Tyler secured her first world title in France before finals day wearing her

Tyler Wright · 169

brother's number 3 jersey and riding a wave goofy foot in his honour.

If her maiden world title had been a runaway, its defence turned out to be more difficult although just as impressive for a different reason. Thought to be out of the race after she injured her knee in Europe, Tyler pressed through the pain. She surfed the final three events in a knee brace with a badly torn MCL and pulled an incredible come-from-behind victory in the final two events of the season to claim number two title. It seemed as though the roll might continue.

Just before the start of the 2018 season Wright was driving north to the Gold Coast when she saw a poster for a music festival on the Central Coast and decided to spend the night listening to some of her favourite musicians, including Amy Shark and Alex the Astronaut. After the show she was introduced to Alex (whose full name is Alexandra Lynn) and the sparks began to fly. Obsessed with surfing from such an early age, Tyler had never paused to think much about her sexuality beyond the possibility that she was bisexual. She had dated boys but she also knew she was attracted to women, although she didn't know how much until she met Lynn. The

Thought to be out of the race after she injured her knee in Europe, Tyler pressed through the pain.

two were immediately inseparable and Tyler was completely accepted into Alex's music world. It was more difficult in Tyler's world, but without making a big deal of it they became known as an item.

In July Tyler and Alex both flew to South Africa. Tyler was competing at Jeffreys Bay, but ahead of that they were going to enjoy a three-day safari. By the time they landed at Port Elizabeth Tyler was feeling sick, and in the hotel she ached all over and couldn't get warm. She began to slip in and out of consciousness. Alex put her in the car and drove her two hours to the nearest hospital. Tyler could barely stand when they arrived at the emergency room.

Diagnosed with influenza A, she was given antibiotics and sent away. She pulled out of the contest, and when her fever broke 10 days later the couple flew home to Australia. 'But I just didn't get better,' Wright told ESPN. Day by day Wright's world closed in around her. The woman known for her power and pain tolerance now struggled to lift her body out of bed. She lost weight, suffered severe memory lapses and delusions, forgot to eat, slept for only a few hours each night and frequently passed out mid-conversation.

After months she was finally diagnosed with post-viral syndrome, a poorly understood condition similar to chronic fatigue. She spent a year in bed, with Alex as her full-time carer, and began to believe there would be no recovery. In June 2019 Dr Brett Jarosz, a sports and exercise chiropractor who had treated Tyler in the past and had worked with post-viral patients, flew to the South Coast to see her. After a brief examination he said: 'To this date, it was the worst post-viral exam I have seen.'

As well as beginning therapy with Jarosz, Wright began a limbic retraining program that targeted her negative fear triggers through exposure, mindfulness and visualisation. For the first time in

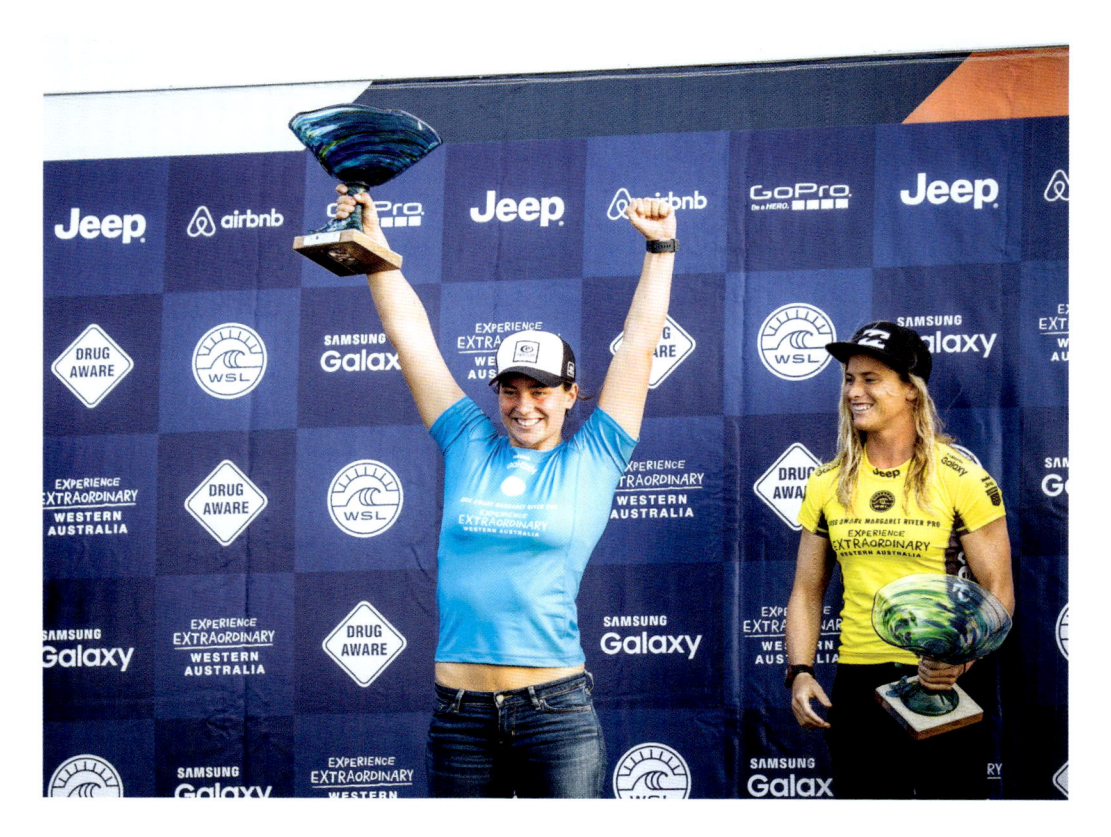

Winning the Drug Aware Pro, Margaret River, Western Australia, 2016. Photo Joli.

Enjoying a free surf at Off the Wall, North Shore, Oahu, 2010. Photo Joli.

her life, in sessions with a therapist and other times with Jarosz, Lynn or members of her family, she allowed her emotional trauma to flow: her past injuries, Owen's accident, her mother's brain tumours, her issues with her father and the fears surrounding her illness. Not quite two months after her initial exam with Dr Jarosz, Wright plunged into the water at Duranbah while her family and Alex looked on. Fourteen months later and 18 kilograms lighter than at her last surf, her wetsuit dangled off an emaciated frame – but she caught 10 waves that morning, reporting to Jarosz on the beach after every three or four before collapsing exhausted on the sand. It was a start.

By November Tyler had advanced enough to return to competition for the last event of the 2019 season on Maui, where amazingly she finished second to Steph Gilmore. Who knew what might happen in 2020? As it turned out, none of us.

In Wright's profile on the WSL website is a dignified, carefully worded description of Tyler Wright's coming out: 'In the years since her illness, Tyler also decided to be more true to herself. She identified as bisexual, wore a pride jersey in the 2021 Maui Pro, and has used her platform as a World Champion to demand equality for women, the LGBTQ+ community, and for minority groups and indigenous people.'

Sadly, her relationship with Alex Lynn did not survive the profound changes she experienced during her recovery, but in every other way she has demonstrated an ongoing commitment to seeking a better, fairer world for all. Nothing demonstrates this better than her taking a knee at the 2020 Tweed Coast Pro, an Australian grand slam event held during the COVID-19 hiatus of the WSL tour.

As her heat began, Wright dropped to one knee on the shoreline and held the position for 439 seconds, one for each of the First Nations people who have died in police custody since 1991. 'Before I'm an athlete, I'm a human being,' she wrote in a statement posted on Instagram. 'These are divisive times and I'm a long way from perfect, but I deeply believe in the pursuit of racial justice and equality for everyone.'

The World Surf League stood behind Wright: 'The WSL is in full support of Wright and everyone around the world who are [sic] making their voices heard against racism and injustice. Surfing is for everyone and the WSL stands in solidarity to proactively work against racism and fight for true equality.'

In an abbreviated world tour in 2021, Wright finished equal sixth on the rankings after winning the Maui Pro again. It was her best result since her 2017 world title, but in 2022 she was still below the finals series cut line with one event to go despite winning Bells and finishing second at Jeffreys Bay.

It was a tough year in other ways too, with brother Owen missing the mid-season cut and possibly bringing down the curtain on his career, while the Wright family's long-term book-keeper was found guilty of embezzling more than $1.5 million from the family over 12 years, more than 80 percent of it belonging to Owen and Tyler. The court was read a letter from Owen suggesting that his parents had been accomplices, further dividing this once-tight surfing family.

But Tyler Wright is nothing if not a fighter, and after showing glimpses of her best during 2022, she was ready to take on the world in 2023.

HONOURABLE MENTIONS

Now comes the really, really hard part.

As I explained in the introduction to this book, my list of the Immortals of surfing is highly subjective but it is based on criteria that widens rather than narrows the scope for inclusion. It would have been easy to say if a surfer had won a world title then they were an Immortal, except then there'd be a very long list of Immortals that did not include some of Australian surfing's most revered heroes.

This is why Gelding Street Press's idea of adding the same number of honourable mentions is a very good one, but what do you say to a world champion who doesn't even rate an honourable mention? Possibly nothing, for the rest of our lives, and there are more than a few in this category. What do you say to Peter Drouyn, Cheyne Horan or Gary Elkerton, none of whom won an open world title, made the list or got an honourable mention but whose contributions to Australian surfing are immeasurable? Only one thing: 'Sorry.'

Phyllis O'Donell (b. 1937)

Perhaps the only world champion to have spun her way to a title, Phyllis O'Donell came to surfing late and won her one and only world championship just four years later, defeating the highly fancied Californian Linda Benson by performing spinners, or turnarounds, at the first amateur world championships at Manly in May 1964.

The mercurial O'Donell, tiny, animated and glowing golden with fake tan all her life, claimed that the jazz she could hear being amplified from the beach on finals day in front of 65,000 people got her in the groove and she just danced and spun her way to victory. However, her historic win in the inaugural world championships was no fluke. She remained a force in women's surfing for the next half dozen years, winning back-to-back Australian titles and finishing third in the 1968 world titles in Puerto Rico and winning several national titles.

Born in Sydney in 1937, she started surfing in 1960 and became

Phyllis O'Donell accepts her trophy after winning the women's division of the Australian Invitational, Bondi, 1963. Photo Bob Weeks.

a regular at Manly, where she was mentored by the legendary Charles 'Snow' McAlister. She moved to Banora Point on the Queensland border in 1963 and honed her skills on the perfect point breaks of Coolangatta. Phyllis had shunned competitive surfing, but in early 1964 Snow turned up in Banora Point and insisted on driving her back to Sydney to compete in the Australian titles. She surprised everyone – not least herself – by winning the nationals, and gained entry into the first world championships.

Smooth stylist Linda Benson of California was widely recognised as the world's best female surfer in 1964, but Phyllis O'Donell was not the least intimidated. There was no denying O'Donell's natural talent, but her public appeal was always in her free-spirited approach and the sheer joy she seemed to derive from every wave. By her own admission, though, Phyllis later became a tough competitor, paddling her opponents down and dispensing colourful verbal abuse to anyone who got in her way.

Now well into her 80s, Phyllis swims most days at a pool near her home and remains vitally interested in the world of surf. She was inducted into the Australian Surfing Hall of Fame in 1996.

Bob McTavish (b. 1944)

One of the most endearing yet controversial characters in Australian surfing, Bob McTavish was born in Mackay, Queensland but moved south to Brisbane with his family before starting high school. While based in surfless Brisbane the teenage McTavish hitchhiked to the coasts in the south or north every chance he got. By the age of 15 he was an accomplished surfer with an original style and a carefree attitude that made every surf a pleasure.

McTavish made his way to Sydney, where Brookvale, near Manly, had just become home to a group of serious surfboard manufacturers. Young Bob knew very little about building boards, but he landed a job as a sander and soon worked his way around the 'Brookvale Six' as he learned the craft. Perpetually broke, McTavish ate a spider for a beer or drank mud from a puddle for a bite of a pie. After spending a summer living in an abandoned car parked by the North Avalon

Bob McTavish at 70, still in total control. Photo McTavish Surfboards.

The Immortals of Australian Surfing · 176

sandhills, he pulled his biggest stunt to date when he stowed away on the Hawaii-bound *Orsova* with a surfer mate. They spent a month surfing on Oahu's North Shore before the long arm of the law descended upon them and they were deported.

By the mid-1960s McTavish was back in Queensland, where he shaped boards and spent much of his time developing his skills in the perfect and little-known waves of Noosa Heads. With such precision waves to ride he was able to develop his surfing and board-design theories and establish what became known as the 'involvement school'. Along with top surfers Nat Young, Russell Hughes and Californian knee boarder George Greenough, McTavish pioneered an approach to surfing that focused on riding close to the curling wave at all times rather than on performing tricks on the flat shoulder. In short, it was riding the wave rather than riding the board.

In 1967 McTavish started to reduce the length of his boards and propel them with a thick, V-shaped hull. The McTavish 'Plastic Machine' made its appearance in Hawaii late in 1967 and the whole surfing world sat up and took notice. These were the first salvos fired in the shortboard revolution that shook the surf world during 1968 and forever changed it.

Although he was several times Queensland champion and a frequent finalist in the nationals, McTavish's heart was never in competing. In the 1970s he opted for a rural lifestyle near Byron Bay, where he continued to shape cutting-edge surfboards while raising a family. When the longboard renaissance began in the 1980s the man who had made them redundant 20 years earlier became the leading supplier to surfers who lacked the desire and the ability to go vertical.

Gail Couper (b. 1947)

Seldom recognised appropriately for the impact she had on Australian women's surfing over more than a decade, Gail Couper is more often remembered as the daughter of feisty but dedicated surfing bureaucrat Stan Couper, president of the Australian Surfriders Association in the 1960s and long-time contest director of the Bells Beach Easter Classic.

While Dad was running the show, Gail was normally winning it. Between 1964 and 1977 she won 14 Victorian state titles, five national titles, an amazing 10 Bells titles and made the finals of the 1966 world championships.

Gail Couper on her way to winning the Bells Beach Easter Classic, 1966. Photo Barrie Sutherland.

Gail started surfing in the early 1960s with friend and Lorne neighbour Wayne Lynch. Although almost five years younger than her Lynch was an early inspiration to Couper, who later claimed that she probably would not have persevered without his encouragement. The rugged west coast of Victoria is famous for big waves and cold water, not the ideal environment for a young girl to get started, but Gail soon learned to hold her own with the boys and was the only woman game to tackle big Bells Beach.

By 1967 Gail was an accomplished surfer in all conditions, but she had made big waves her own. No woman surfer looked as relaxed in the big stuff until Layne Beachley started riding mountains in the late 1990s. The Bells Classic of 1967 was held in big, powerful waves, and the women's division was a one-horse race. Gail so intimidated her opposition with her fearless take-offs that she was never threatened by anyone again when she competed at Bells.

In her 20s Couper's teaching career took precedence over competitive surfing, but she still managed most of the major contests in Australia. Wherever she surfed she was the woman to beat, and at Bells she was invincible.

Terry Fitzgerald (b. 1950)

A sickly child who spent almost a year in hospital with osteomyelitis, Terry Fitzgerald was a late bloomer as a surfer and only really became interested when he watched the television coverage of the first world surfing championships at Manly in 1964 as a 14 year old. From there it was a very fast track to greatness, first hinted at in 1970 at the world titles in Victoria where he impressed with his long, carving speed lines and only just failed to make the final.

Fitzgerald grew up in Maroubra on Sydney's eastern beaches. Despite his childhood health issues, he was a good student and an all-round sportsman who represented his school in rugby. He seemed destined for a conventional career, until he watched Midget Farrelly at Manly and saw the light. The following Christmas, Terry and his brother were given surfboards.

After little more than a year of surfing on his own board Fitzgerald finished second in his first

Terry Fitzgerald, 1978. Photo courtesy Quiksilver.

competitive outing, the New South Wales school boys titles. Around that time the family moved across town to Collaroy, and the surfing epicentre of North Narrabeen became his new base. While his surfing continued to improve, Terry struggled at first to adapt to the new shortboards until, soon after finishing school in 1967, he got a 7-feet full concave. The vivid orange board went like a freight train and Terry became known as the 'orange speed blur', the first of many nicknames that related to his penchant for speed on a surfboard.

Fitzgerald moved to the Gold Coast in late 1968, bluffed his way into Joe Larkin's surfboard factory and learned to shape. He was a natural and was soon highly regarded in the industry for his fine-lined speed shapes. The following year he went to Hawaii for the first time. The powerful North Shore waves were perfect for his long, arc turns and he soon became part of the Lightning Bolt/Dick Brewer push, probably the most advanced surfboard designers in the world at that time. The legendary Brewer took the Aussie under his wing and helped fine-tune his shaping, which left Fitzgerald well equipped to branch out on his own back in Sydney, where he opened Hot Buttered Surfboards at the end of 1971.

After winning at Bells Beach in 1972 Fitzgerald suddenly seemed unstoppable as a competitor, and in the early years of pro surfing he often equalled Michael Peterson as the most exciting surfer to watch. Fitz won several major events in Hawaii over this period but he also became a regular in Tahiti and on secret islands of the Micronesian chain. In 1975 he discovered South Africa's Jeffreys Bay. The freight-train barrels seemed tailor-made for his style, and it was there he was given his lasting nom de board: the 'sultan of speed'.

Peter Townend (b. 1953)

The first world champion of the pro era won his 1976 title without winning a single event, and for much of his career he was destined to finish somewhere on the podium but not on the top rung. Nonetheless, he was one of the most admired and flamboyant surfers on the tour: technically precise and consistent but capable of moments of great showmanship.

Townend, who became universally known by his initials 'PT' very early in his career, was born

Peter Townend, Rocky Point, Hawaii, 1977. Photo Dan Merkel.

on the Gold Coast and raised at Coolangatta. By the mid-1960s he was an accomplished longboarder, but he did not make a competitive impact until after the shortboard breakthrough. By the start of the 1970s, however, as part of the 'Coolangatta Kids' push along with Michael Peterson and Rabbit Bartholomew, he had started to define himself as a surfer and drew smooth lines along the point waves of Snapper Rocks and Kirra.

In 1971 he also began to define himself as a competitor, finishing second as a junior in the Australian titles then starting a four-year run of seconds in the senior division the following year. Townend's consistency paid off when he made the Australian team for the San Diego world titles in 1972, finishing the highest-placed Australian with a third. By then he was considered to be a small-wave stylist, the 'four foot and under man' as one writer put it.

In 1974 PT crushed the 4-feet myth by contesting the final of the Smirnoff Pro in monster Waimea Bay storm surf. He finished fourth but managed to impress everyone with some calm, methodical and flawless drops down 30-feet faces. Suddenly a celebrity, he came home and threw himself enthusiastically into the development of the Australian

Honourable mentions · 181

Professional Surfers Association and a new 'rock star' persona.

During 1976 Hawaiian event promoters Fred Hemmings and Randy Rarick managed to pull together a structure for an international pro tour to be known as International Professional Surfing, but the fact that a new tour existed did not become public until it was almost finished. When the new points allocations for each result were tallied it came as a surprise to many that Peter Townend was the first official world professional surfing champion. No one who understood basic maths could detract from Townend's victory, as he had simply done what every touring pro has to do: perform consistently well throughout the season.

Townend and 1976 number two Ian Cairns went on to form marketing troupe the Bronzed Aussies, which was basically an extension of PT's rock-star dream. In the 1980s Townend and Cairns moved to California and successfully ran the National Scholastic Surfing Association for several years, nurturing such talents as Tom Curren and Brad Gerlach. Townend subsequently developed a successful career in publishing, media and marketing in the US, where he still lives.

Wayne Bartholomew (b. 1954)

Australia's second world professional champion, in 1978, Gold Coaster Wayne 'Rabbit' Bartholomew was one of the most explosive performers on the world pro tour from its inception in 1976 through to the end of the 1980s. He was also its leading grommet, a Peter Pan type who never let go of his urchin ways despite considerable fame and fortune.

The second child of a schoolmaster and a dance teacher, Bartholomew was soon followed by three younger sisters. When his parents' marriage broke down and his mother left the family home with five kids in tow, Rabbit (so named originally for his ability to dart across the field at junior soccer) escaped the constraints of an all-female household by spending his days surfing Greenmount Point on borrowed boards and frequenting the pinball parlours of Coolangatta. Betty Bartholomew struggled to put food on the table, and Rabbit soon turned to petty theft along the beach to support her.

By 1968 Rabbit had a board of his own and had begun to surf competitively. When the family moved house again up the coast a few kilometres to Kirra, he also had to come to terms with the infamous Kirra barrel. Rabbit and neighbour Michael Peterson, along with Peter Townend and occasionally goofy footer Andrew McKinnon, became known as the 'Coolie Kids', even though they were spread out along the coast from Burleigh to Snapper Rocks.

In 1972 the Coolie Kids all made the Australian team for the world titles in San Diego, where Townend finished third. Rabbit and Peterson stopped over in Hawaii on the way home, and Rabbit got his first taste of North Shore power. The big waves scared and thrilled him at the same time, and he instinctively felt that Hawaii would be a special place in his growth as a surfer. By 1975

Rabbit Bartholomew busting down the door at Pipeline, 1975. Photo Dan Merkel.

Bartholomew was at the forefront of a movement known as the 'backside attack' on Pipeline's hard-breaking left-hand barrels. Along with fellow Australians Townend, Ian Cairns and Mark Richards and South Africans Shaun and Michael Tomson, Rabbit pioneered a gutsy new style of riding the world's most dangerous wave.

With the advent of a world professional tour in 1976 Rabbit became one of its strongest advocates, and after winning his world title he became a mentor to many of the younger surfers who joined the tour. Although he won only a few more tour events – he won a career total of eight – after Mark Richards began his twin-finned dominance, he remained a threat until his retirement in 1988.

In the 1990s Rabbit became increasingly involved in surfing administration and in 1999 began a nine-year reign as head of the Association of Surfing Professionals, moving their headquarters back to his own backyard at Coolangatta.

Mark Stewart (b. 1963)

Although 'Mono' has won just about every adaptive title going – regional, national and international – since they were introduced, he has also had some spectacular near misses.

He missed out on a third consecutive world AS2 (amputee class) title at the International Surfing Association Championships at La Jolla, California in 2017, for example, even though things were looking good going into the quarter finals.

Mono, who surfs on one knee on a scooped-out board designed by kneeboard legend George Greenough to accommodate his stump, revels in a bit of power, and that was what was on offer that morning. Then it all went pear-shaped. 'My arms gave way on me,' Mono messaged friends. 'Couldn't feel them. Then I passed out on the beach.' He spent the night in hospital undergoing tests, but released himself against medical advice the following morning to surf the final – and almost won it. No one who knows the Mono story was surprised.

When he was 15 years old and a star soccer striker, Mark Stewart slid into the goalmouth to get a touch around the keeper and instead got his leg wedged between the goalie and the goalpost. The fiery youngster, who had already made a name for himself at Main Beach and The Pass as a charger, was stretchered off the ground and the coach insisted he get the injury checked out.

Mono tucks into a Bali barrel. Photo courtesy Mark Stewart.

The day after having X-rays at Lismore Hospital Mono and his mother flew to Sydney, where he was given a biopsy and other tests. The day after that his right leg was amputated at the thigh, but Mono was neither depressed nor angry. 'I couldn't afford to be, because I had to focus everything in me on surviving the chemo, and in those days it was brutal.' Typically, Mono took the loss of his leg as something to give thanks for, because his local doctor had recognised his osteosarcoma and saved his life. Despite the many setbacks and frustrations, Mono has never stopped giving thanks or giving back to the handicapped community.

As the chemotherapy came to an end another amputee surfer suggested Mono try customising a kneeboard, and within a few weeks he was hopping to the water's edge and paddling out to carve the ferocious hacks he would become famous for.

Although the para movement has been part of many sports for decades, surfing was slow to adapt. To his great credit, International Surfing Association (ISA) boss Fernando Aguerre made it his personal mission to introduce adaptive surfing around the world. In September 2015, at the age of 51, Mark Mono Stewart became the inaugural ISA world adaptive surfing champion.

Barton Lynch on a big clean day at home at Barrenjoey, 2001. Photo Aitionn.

When his cancer returned in 2021 Mono decided to contest one of his favourite events, the Hawaiian championships, more as a farewell to old friends than anything else, but old habits die hard. He flew to Hawaii in a break during chemotherapy sessions to reduce a large tumour in his neck, decided to compete anyway and won by the slimmest of margins. It was the bravest victory in a career that is far from over.

Barton Lynch (b. 1963)

Like his friend, fellow goofy-foot and pro-tour contemporary Damien Hardman, Barton Lynch was frequently underrated, usually at the peril of those who failed to understand his tactical brilliance. But unlike Hardman, throughout his career Lynch was a magnificently honest and frank observer of the pro scene who always had an outrageous sound bite for the TV crew or a shocking headline for the newspaper.

Lynch grew up in Whale Beach at the trendy end of Sydney's Northern Beaches and started surfing in the early 1970s. By the end of the decade he was recognised as a grom with a future, but in an era when super heroes ruled the Newport Peak and Narrabeen there wasn't much room for a skinny, adenoidal kid from Whaley to leave a mark.

All that changed in 1981 when Barton finished second in the national juniors. In 1983, the year he turned pro, he won the coveted pro junior title, usually considered a signal of great things to come. A clever tactician from the beginning, he used psychological ploys, impeccable timing and a keen wave sense to defeat his opponents. Never at any time in his career was he the best surfer in the world, but he was often the cleverest.

After finishing 13th in his rookie year, Lynch made the top 10 in 1984 and was runner-up to Tom Curren in 1985. He couldn't maintain the pace and many had written him off when he made a spectacularly late run for the title in 1988. He was third going into the season closer, the Billabong Pro at Pipeline, behind Hardman and Tom Carroll. The surf was big and perfect, and all three contenders were barrel-riding goofy footers. Unbelievably, Carroll and Hardman went out in the early rounds and BL stormed home. It was an amazing season end not to be repeated for another decade, and finally Barton Lynch had the world's attention.

BL went on to enjoy a long and consistently high-ranked pro-tour career, with 17 world tour wins to his credit. He never won a second title but he used his 1988 crown to great effect, forging a media career and becoming one of surfing's most outspoken elder statesmen and an effective tour representative for the pros.

Damien Hardman (b. 1966)

For a man with two world title trophies on his shelf, Damien 'Dooma' Hardman is perhaps the most uncelebrated of Australia's truly great surfers. The fault is not his. Like so many Australian sporting champions before him, Hardman never sought the limelight nor courted the media: he liked to blend into the crowd.

Left with few personal morsels to pick over, the media found he was a winning machine who was light on soul and character. None of this was true or fair, but you could see where it was coming from because Hardman's precision surfing was rather like Ivan Lendl's baseline play: unbeatable but tragically predictable. It came as no surprise that Dooma's sporting hero was Lendl.

When you looked at Hardman's individual moves there was great beauty in them. He carved a lovely backside bottom turn, for example, and then he did it again and again.

But if Hardman's surfing lacked the explosive drama of a Gary Elkerton or a Martin Potter that mattered little to the man himself, who was methodically moving towards a world title from the day he joined the tour.

Born in Sydney, Hardman grew up close to the power-surf centre of Narrabeen, where he started surfing at age 10 and was soon learning from the likes of Terry Fitzgerald, Col Smith and Simon Anderson. At 16 Hardman came third in the national juniors at his home beach and gave notice of what was to come. Having left school in 1984, he won the national juniors and went on to win the junior world title at Huntington Beach, California.

On tour full time in 1985 he finished in the middle of the field, but in 1986 he pushed into the top 10 early and finished at number six. He was then a contender, but still very few saw it coming. In 1987 he consistently posted the results he needed and claimed the title in the season closer at

Damien Hardman at Bells Beach, 1992. Photo Joli.

The Immortals of Australian Surfing · 188

Age shall not weary him: Occy down the line hard during Cyclone Oma, 2019. Photo Joli.

Manly up against Gary Elkerton. Dooma versus Kong was a battle of the extremes, method versus madness, and in this instance sanity prevailed. It was close enough to a hometown win for the crowd to be happy and everyone liked the affable Hardman, but there was also considerable disappointment, particularly in the media, that the wild and woolly Elkerton's flamboyant style had yet again not been rewarded.

Mr Consistency stayed in the top five for the next six years, winning his second world title in 1990. Although he faded somewhat in the 1990s, Hardman remained on tour until 2001 and notched 19 tour victories in a stellar career.

Mark Occhilupo (b. 1966)

He is possibly Australia's most revered surfer, a vulnerable, child-like figure whose extraordinary career spanned more than two decades and encompassed more radical highs and lows than anyone else in sport. 'Occy' was a child prodigy who had to wait until he was 33 to win a world title, in what has been described as one of the most remarkable comebacks in any sport.

Born in southern Sydney, Occhilupo started surfing before he'd reached his teens and developed his skills quickly by copying every move of his hero, Tom Carroll. Like Carroll, Occy was a slightly built kid but he had powerful legs and a low centre of

Honourable mentions · 189

gravity approach to surfing. In the early days it wasn't pretty, but Occy soon developed finesse and began to learn where the speed section of the wave was and how to get there.

Occy quit school at the age of 17 and joined the pro tour in 1983, finishing 16th in his rookie year. The following year he looked a more complete surfer, with a fluid backhand attack being his signature. He finished the season at number three in the world, picking up the world pro junior title as a bonus. Over the next couple of seasons, while the world title eluded him, Occy became a brilliant competitor, tactically shrewd and able to put together a winning heat much of the time. Carroll had his measure and so did the next champion, Tom Curren. Nevertheless, Occy won five events in 1985 and became Australia's favourite surfer.

By 1987, however, all was clearly not well with Mark Occhilupo. His behaviour had become erratic, he started drinking heavily and using cocaine and spent months at a time as a couch potato, watching television while consuming massive quantities of junk food. Unsurprisingly, his body blew up to more than 120 kilograms, and on his rare trips to the surf the bloated Occy was a tragic figure.

Diagnosed with bipolar disorder in the early 1990s, Occhilupo spent more than a year in therapy. Filmmaker Jack McCoy took him on filming trips on the understanding that he'd keep the camera away from him until he'd lost weight, a confidence-building exercise that worked. Occy rejoined the world tour in 1997 and finished the season second to Kelly Slater.

After a so-so year in 1998, Occy won three tour events in 1999 and scored highly enough in the others to win the world title by a big margin. After six straight years of Slater dominance, the public and media revelled in the greatest comeback story surfing had ever seen.

Pauline Menczer (b. 1970)

Pauline Menczer never had anything handed to her on a platter. She rose to the top of her field despite all kind of obstacles, and had enough heart to laugh at her misfortunes along the way.

Raised in Sydney's Bondi by her widowed mother after her father and grandfather were killed in separate car accidents just weeks apart, at age five Menczer had no idea how much the double tragedy affected her mother, who had four young children to care

Pauline Menczer wraps up a world title at big Sunset Beach, 1993. Photo Aitionn.

for, but resilience was a quality she developed very early.

Pauline loved the beach and spent a lot of time there, but she didn't try surfing until the age of 12. She quickly developed a gritty, powerful style and a grim determination to win heats and within a few years was one of Australia's leading amateurs. In 1988 she won her first world title at the world amateurs in Puerto Rico.

Joining the pro tour in 1989, Menczer finished her rookie year in third place, dropped to sixth in 1990 and then challenged for the title in 1991, being narrowly beaten by Wendy Botha. Her form was consistent over this period despite the fact that she had developed crippling rheumatoid arthritis in her elbows, wrists and fingers.

In 1993 Menczer put her pain to one side and started the season in devastating form, winning three early events and placing herself in contention for the world title before the arthritis worsened. Although her form suffered, she went into the last event in Hawaii still holding a ratings lead but she needed to surf well to hold it. Two weeks before the season closer she had an arthritis attack so severe that she was in a wheelchair for a week. She paddled out at Sunset Beach into a solid 8-feet surf with no surf training and feeling as weak as a kitten. She paced herself, took long rides and made the final, thereby

Honourable mentions · 191

Sally Fitzgibbons in full flight at the Rip Curl Search, Puerto Rico, 2010. Photo Joli.

winning the bravest world title in pro-surfing history.

Menczer also had financial hurdles to get over, confiding that she had spent $25,000 of her $30,000 title-year winnings just to travel the tour, and that included sleeping on the floor in friends' houses rather than paying for hotels. Pauline could make light of the fact that she was without a sponsor for most of her career, but as her string of titles and tour wins grew she found it difficult to understand why she had no commercial value.

Pauline continued on the tour and maintained a top-10 ranking throughout the 1990s, coming second in 1996, while amassing 20 tour victories and eight on the qualifying series, a feat still bettered only by Layne Beachley. In 18 years on tour her winnings totalled less than $450,000, making her average annual income as an unsponsored pro around $25,000.

Menczer just shrugged and got on with creating a new post-tour life, during which she has belatedly received due recognition for her services to the sport.

Sally Fitzgibbons (b. 1990)

As a surfer, smiley-faced Sally Fitzgibbons has taken the aloha spirit into every battle she has fought over a distinguished 14-year career at the top, winning her many friends and admirers in the surfers' area as well as the grandstands. However, the truth is she would have been a crowd pleaser no matter what sport she chose.

Fitzgibbons was a born athlete. From an early age she played soccer and touch football, ran cross country and ended up a national champion middle-distance runner in high school. Ultimately, though, her love for surfing won out.

Sally grew up on the pretty, surf-rich stretch of coast around Gerroa on the south coast of New South Wales, and honed her early skills in the wide variety of sparsely crowded line-ups nearby. She burst onto the competitive scene in 2005 when, at the age of 14, she became the youngest-ever winner of the Billabong Pro Junior. On debut she impressed with an easy flowing style and the ability to produce explosive moves at the right times. She won the International Surfing Association world under-18 title in Portugal at the age of 16, then took the Association of Surfing Professionals world junior championship.

With a wall of positive noise developing around her, at 18 she won the qualifying series championship faster than any woman in history. She then finished her 2009 World Championship Tour rookie season in fifth position on the rankings and went to world number two in 2010. She finished second again in 2011 and 2012, edging closer to her dream – or so we all hoped.

Despite her unbelievable talent as a surfer and her winning personality, you have to feel sorry for Sally Fitzgibbons. Through an accident of birth she landed herself in one of the toughest competitive eras in recent history, and slumped in the rankings while Steph Gilmore, Carissa Moore and Tyler Wright battled it out for titles. She re-emerged in warrior shape in 2017 and wore the yellow jersey most of the year before stumbling on Maui and finishing third. In 2019 she was again on a title run but finished fourth, although her performances were enough to secure a spot on the Australian team for the Tokyo Olympics. Her quarter-finals elimination brought an end to her medal dream, one of her saddest moments in surfing.

Sally came back strongly in the shortened 2021 season, finishing third, but in 2022 she failed to make the mid-season cut. Granted a World Surf League wildcard for 2023, she may yet have a final chance to win that coveted world title.

BIBLIOGRAPHY

Books

Baker, Tim, 2007. *High Surf: The world's most inspiring surfers*, Harper Sports, Sydney.

Baker, Tim, 2011. *Surf for Your Life: Mick Fanning*, Penguin Books, Sydney.

Baker, Tim and Anderson, Simon, 2011. *Thrust: The Simon Anderson story*, Surfing World, Sydney.

Baker, Tim and Occhilupo, Mark, 2008. *Occy: The rise and fall and rise of Mark Occhilupo*, Ebury Press, Sydney.

Bartholomew, Wayne Rabbit with Tim Baker, 1996. *Bustin' Down the Door*, Harper Sports, Sydney.

Carroll, Nick, 2013. *TC: Tom Carroll*, Ebury Press, Sydney.

Doherty, Sean, 2004. *MP: The life of Michael Peterson*, Harper Collins, Sydney.

Doherty, Sean, 2015. *MP Untold: The lost stories of an Australian surfing legend*, Nero, Melbourne.

Doherty, Sean, 2020. *Golden Daze: Australian surfing then to now*, Hachette Australia, Sydney.

Farrelly, Midget with Craig McGregor, 1965. *This Surfing Life*, Rigby Books, Adelaide.

Gordon, Michael, 2008. *Layne Beachley: Beneath the waves*, Ebury Press, Sydney.

Jarratt, Phil, 1977. *The Wave Game: An inside look at professional surfing*, Tracks Publishing, Sydney.

Jarratt, Phil, 1997. *Mr Sunset: the Jeff Hakman story*, General Publishing Group, Los Angeles.

Jarratt, Phil, 2006. *The Mountain and the Wave: The Quiksilver Story*, Quiksilver Entertainment, Huntington Beach.

Jarratt, Phil, 2010. *Salts and Suits: How a bunch of surf bums created a multi-billion dollar industry*, Hardie Grant, Melbourne.

Jarratt, Phil, 2011. *Australia's Hottest 100 Surfing Legends*, Hardie Grant, Melbourne.

Jarratt, Phil, 2012 and 2017. *Surfing Australia: A complete history of surfboard riding in Australia*, Hardie Grant, Melbourne.

Jarratt, Phil and Neil Jameson, Neil (eds), 1984. *Wide World of Sports Australian Sporting Hall of Fame*, Angus & Robertson, Sydney.

McTavish, Bob, 2009. *Stoked!*, Hyams Publishing, Hyams Beach, New South Wales.

McTavish, Bob, 2013. *More Stoked!*, Harper Collins, Sydney.

Stell, Marion K., 1992. *Pam Burridge*, Angus & Robertson, Sydney.

Warshaw, Matt, 2003. *The Encyclopedia of Surfing*, Harcourt, New York.

Warshaw, Matt, 2010. *The History of Surfing*, Chronicle Books, San Francisco.

Willcox, Kirk, 1994. *Tom Carroll: The wave within*, Ironbark, Sydney.

Young, Nat, 1998. *Nat's Nat and That's That*, Nymboida Press, Sydney.

Magazines

Men's Health (Australia)
Outside (United States)
Surfer (United States)
Surfing World (Australia)
The Australian Women's Weekly
The Bulletin
The Surfer's Journal (United States)
Tracks (Australia)
Vogue Australia
Wahine (United States)

Newspapers

Noosa Today
The Australian
The Manly Daily
The Sydney Morning Herald
The Washington Post

Websites

eos.surf (Encyclopedia of Surfing)
espn.com
60minutes.com.au
surfersjournal.com
surfline.com
swellnet.com
theinertia.com
tracksmag.com.au
worldsurfleague.com

Mick Fanning in the yellow jersey and on fire: Rip Curl Pro, Bells Beach, 2012. Photo Joli.

ACKNOWLEDGEMENTS

First, my sincere thanks to Rockpool Publishing/Gelding Street Press and in particular to its leaders Lisa Hanrahan and Paul Dennett for creating such a fine library of Immortals and giving me the opportunity to write this surfing volume.

Second, thanks to the hands-on crew who got this over the line: Acquisitions Editor Luke West, who has been my guiding light in combining the somewhat renegade nature of the surfing culture with the over-arching philosophy of this Immortals series in honouring the greatest sporting heroes in our history; editor Lisa Macken, whose deft touch has helped refine my crusty old prose.

Third, I thank the members of the fairly small club of Australian surfing historians, of which I am probably the most prolific, but not far behind are my colleagues and friends Tim Baker, Sean Doherty and Nick Carroll and in the US Matt Warshaw, the historian's historian. I also thank the eccentric but lovable bunch of ratbags past and present who have captured our history in a library of such memorable and magical memories.

Finally, thanks to my loving wife and family for putting up yet again with a cranky old author on deadline, and to my surfing mates (particularly those who occasionally buy a book) from around the country and around the world who have made covering this sport, art and culture for more than half a century such a pleasure.

ABOUT THE AUTHOR

Phil Jarratt is a journalist, author, publisher and film-maker with more than 50 years' experience in Australian and international media. Born in Wollongong, New South Wales, he is a former editor of *Tracks*, associate editor of *Surfer* and editor and publisher of *The Australian Surfer's Journal*. He is regarded as being one of the foremost global authorities on surfing and has worked inside the executive ranks of two of the world's biggest surf brands – Rip Curl and Quiksilver – where he was a senior marketing executive for 10 years in Europe and the US.

Phil has written more than 40 books covering sport-related biography, surfing and surf history, travel and youth culture and has been published in the US, UK and France as well as Australia. As a film-maker he has written and produced the documentaries *8 Days of Pure Stoke*, *A Cup of Tea with God*, *Men of Wood & Foam* and *Generation 99*. *Men of Wood & Foam*, made for Foxtel's History Channel, was selected for the 2018 Santa Barbara International Film Festival and won

The author at Cloudbreak, Fiji. Photo Tom Servais.

the Australian Surfing Hall of Fame Media Award in 2016.

Phil has received the Australian Surfing Hall of Fame Media Award five times and was shortlisted for the Blake Dawson Business Literature Prize in 2010 for *Salts and Suits*, a warts and all history of the surf industry that inspired the 2022 ABC drama series *Barons*.

Phil has lived in Noosa for more than 30 years, where he writes for the local newspaper and surfs or paddles every day.

ALSO IN THIS SERIES

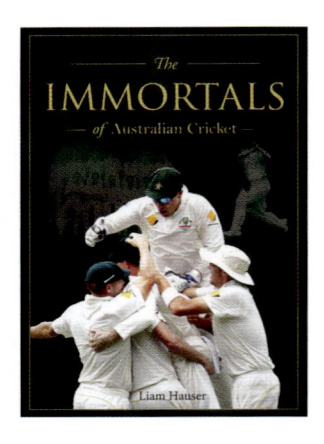

The Immortals of Australian Cricket
by Liam Hauser
ISBN: 9781925682786

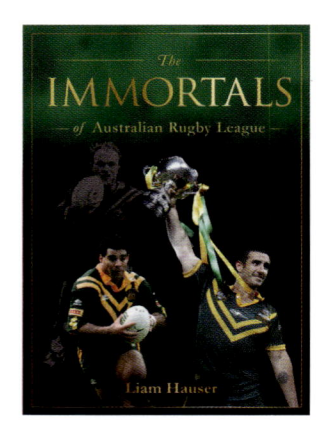

The Immortals of Australian Rugby League
by Liam Hauser
ISBN: 9781925946031

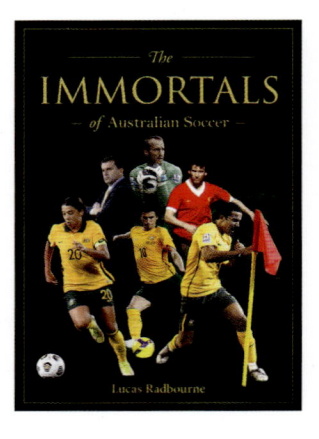

The Immortals of Australian Soccer
by Lucas Radbourne
ISBN: 9781922579355

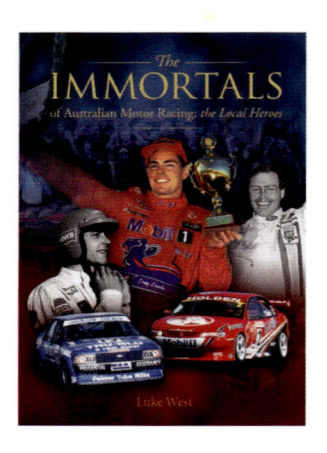

The Immortals of Australian Motor Racing: the Local Heroes
by Luke West
ISBN: 9781925946987

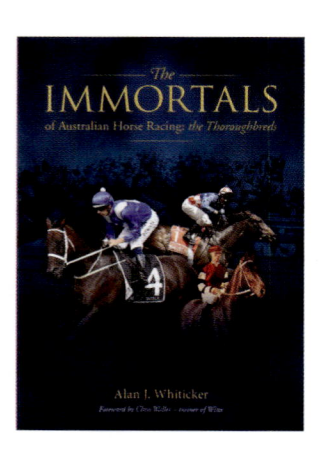

The Immortals of Australian Horse Racing: the Thoroughbreds
by Alan J. Whiticker
ISBN: 9781925946963

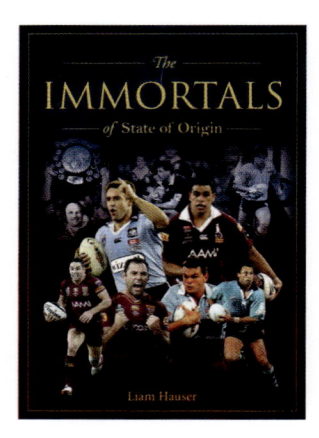

The Immortals of State of Origin
by Liam Hauser
ISBN: 9781922579799

Available now from all good book stores.
Also visit www.geldingstreetpress.com.

IDGET FARRELLY · NAT YOUNG · WA
NDERSON · MARK RICHARDS · TOM
AYNE BEACHLEY · STEPH GILMORE ·
WAYNE LYNCH · MICHAEL PETERSON
ARROLL · MICK FANNING · PAM BUR
TYLER WRIGHT · MIDGET FARRELLY
ETERSON · SIMON ANDERSON · MAR
PAM BURRIDGE · LAYNE BEACHLEY
ARRELLY · NAT YOUNG · WAYNE LYNC
MARK RICHARDS · TOM CARROLL ·
EACHLEY · STEPH GILMORE · TYLER
AYNE LYNCH · MICHAEL PETERSON
ARROLL · MICK FANNING · PAM BUR
TYLER WRIGHT · MIDGET FARRELLY
ETERSON · SIMON ANDERSON · MAR
PAM BURRIDGE · LAYNE BEACHLEY
ARRELLY · NAT YOUNG · WAYNE LYNC
MARK RICHARDS · TOM CARROLL ·
EACHLEY · STEPH GILMORE · TYLER
AYNE LYNCH · MICHAEL PETERSON
ARROLL · MICK FANNING · PAM BUR
TYLER WRIGHT · MIDGET FARRELLY